# God's Man In the Family

**THE NINE ESSENTIALS**

*Caring For the Ones You Love*

## FLOYD McCLUNG, JR.

**HARVEST HOUSE PUBLISHERS**
Eugene, Oregon 97402

**GOD'S MAN IN THE FAMILY**

Copyright © 1994 by Floyd McClung, Jr.
Published by Harvest House Publishers
Eugene, Oregon 97402

Library of Congress Cataloging-in-Publication Data

McClung, Floyd.
    God's man in the family / Floyd McClung.
      p.    cm.
    ISBN 0-89081-881-9
    1. Fathers—Religious life.    2. Fatherhood (Christian theology).
I. Title.
BV4846.M35   1994                       93-31614
248.8'421—dc20                              CIP

**Printed in the United States of America.**

94  95  96  97  98  99  00  –  10  9  8  7  6  5  4  3  2  1

*To Dad, who's always been*
*God's man in my family.*
*Thank you, Dad!*

# WITH GRATEFUL APPRECIATION

I'd like to express my thanks to Bob Hawkins, Sr., Bob Hawkins, Jr., and Eileen Mason, who were patient with me when I was a year and a half behind in submitting this manuscript. Thanks for your forgiveness when I failed to keep my deadlines, and for believing in me enough to introduce me to a wonderful writer by the name of Steve Halliday, who helped draw out of me the stories and principles that I so firmly believe in and who helped get my bumbling words onto paper. Thank you all for believing in me and making this book possible!

And thank you, Sally, for being the best wife a guy could ever have. I haven't always felt like God's man in the family, but you've always believed in me and encouraged me. Thanks, Babe!

# CONTENTS

# WHAT ARE YOUR NONNEGOTIABLES?

Fatherhood is one of those skills no one goes to school to learn. And not many of us had dads who trained us in the art and practice of fatherhood. Yet one of the most important things we can do is to raise children. We can damage them, hurt them, and inhibit them, or encourage them, strengthen them, and send them out to succeed. It's an unimaginably important role, yet it's an area of life for which we lack training.

In order to be the man in the family God wants us to be, we need a plan. Being God's man is a long-term project, and we need to begin with the end in sight. What kind of family do we want? What kind of man do we want to be?

Some people give hard-and-fast rules for being a godly man. In fact, some preachers and teachers hand out rule books and give you the impression that if you just obey the rules, everything will fall into place. If that is what you are looking for in this book, you are looking in the wrong place. I don't think life works that way.

You can program a computer to do certain things on command, but don't try it with human beings! We are far too complex to act like machines. Besides, God wants to teach us wisdom and discernment, not Pavlovian reactions like dogs who salivate when they hear the dinner bell.

So, rather than merely give rules to obey, what I will try to offer you in this book are life-tested, biblical principles. They do not guarantee you success, but they will help you become a mature disciple of Jesus. Rules focus on outward performance. Principles have to do with our character, with who we are as men.

If this is the vision that inspires you (and I certainly hope it is), then I believe I can help you on the path toward becoming God's man in the family. It is a *process*, a lifetime process, but at least we'll know what we are building toward. This is a vision worth sacrificing for, to keep us going in tough times: to be a man of character, a man of God, who is committed to being all God wants him to be—*God's man* in the family.

A second reason I wrote this book is to help you think through the "nonnegotiables" that will shape who you become as husband and father. What rock-solid, unchanging values and principles will shape your interaction with your family?

## MY PERSONAL JOURNEY

It's harder for some to discover their nonnegotiables than it is for others. On a personal level, I was fortunate. I had a great father and I learned many of my nonnegotiable principles for being a godly father and husband from him.

Dad was a pastor, so my family's social circle, worship circle, and work circle were all integrated. I used to think that was bad, but I've changed my mind in the last few years. Even though dad was very busy, he was around a lot. Our home did not face the kind of disintegration many of our neighbors faced.

Families today normally work in one place, socialize in another place, worship in another place, shop in another place, and live in yet another place—and none of those worlds are connected. Our family was not being pulled in a million directions.

In high school, I played sports, had a small circle of friends who had good parents, then went to a Christian college. I was oblivious to the stresses rampant in the general culture.

That all changed in 1967. On June 1 I graduated from college and the next day Sally and I were married. Three days later we led an outreach with 90 young people into the West Indies. We slept with a sheet between us and 30 screaming teenage girls.

Life was certainly exciting for us, even though it was seldom easy! I wanted to be a good husband, but I soon found out I had a lot to learn. Since those days Sally and I have gone through a lot of healing in our relationship because we entered marriage without any understanding of communication. Nobody sat us down and gave us premarital counseling. I understood nothing about kindness and expressing my emotions and drawing my wife out and listening—really listening—to her. None of that was a part of my world.

## JILTED EXPECTATIONS

My sky-high expectations didn't make it any easier on our marriage. I wanted Sally to be Mother Teresa, Betty Crocker, and Elizabeth Taylor all rolled into one. In fact, the first morning of our marriage I actually said to her, "Would you mind serving me breakfast in bed?"

That had always been my dream, my cherished fantasy...and Sally laughed at me! I knew then that I was in trouble. "I've never cooked breakfast in my life," she giggled as my dreamworld shattered into a pile of cold cereal.

Sally's expectations differed from my own. An older woman told her before our wedding that she and her husband had never spoken a cross word to each other in 14 years. We found out later it was a big lie—they simply didn't talk. But Sally adopted the expectation that we would not argue.

Now, I've got Irish blood flowing in my veins and I raise my voice when I'm upset. For almost two years, I said things in such a way that I hurt Sally very deeply. She kept all the pain inside while I just cruised along, oblivious to what was happening between us.

Until Jamaica. Sally and I went there with Youth With A Mission (YWAM) to work with college kids on a summer outreach. One night we had a huge blowup. For several bitter hours Sally unloaded on me all the hurts from the first two years of our marriage. I thought we were going to get divorced—I honestly thought it was the end of the road for us. And the end of my world.

## WISDOM OUT OF DESPERATION

Out of desperation, we began to cry out for wisdom. If we were to save our marriage, we had to learn how to relate to each other. I had to discover what it meant to be a good husband. I started searching for biblical principles on which to build our marriage. I sought counsel, I read Christian books, I searched the

Scriptures, and I talked about it with my dear (and sometimes bewildered) wife.

My schooling continued when Sally and I went with Youth With A Mission to pioneer a halfway house in Kabul, Afghanistan, for drugged-out European and American kids. Those were the hippie days. Martin Luther King, Jr. had just been assassinated, the Vietnam War was in full swing, and Richard Nixon was taking over the White House. Kids fled the country by the planeload.

All of a sudden I ran into the reality of the twentieth century, and it blew me away. Here I was at the age of 25 working with the mixed-up products of western, industrialized society. I had no idea these kids existed— long-haired, doped-up, hostile to their parents' values, and desperately searching for meaning. They came from upper-middle class families, where they had been bought off, and every one of them was messed up.

At the time I thought the frustrated, disillusioned American kids we were dealing with were an exception. But I changed my mind when I returned to the United States. The kids we dealt with in Afghanistan were *typical*; both they and their parents were in serious trouble.

That experience reinforced for me how important it was to be the kind of man God wanted me to be—both for my wife and, one day, for my kids.

Jamaica and Afghanistan were watersheds in my life. They made up the two major crises that most powerfully shaped my desire to be a good husband and father. Out of those personal dilemmas, the pain Sally and I inflicted on each other, and the pain we saw in the lives of the kids we were ministering to, I determined, "I'm going to be a father to my kids and a husband to my

> *I wanted to be the kind of
> man who inspired his wife
> and children to love God
> and trust Him.*

wife. I'm going to figure out what this means and what values to live by—whatever it takes." I had a healthy fear of failure and was overwhelmed by my inadequacy ...but I was too stubborn to give up.

## THE NONNEGOTIABLES COME TOGETHER

From these experiences I determined to find the things that would help me be the man God wanted me to be in my family.

I decided that a man needed above all things to be *godly*, and that godliness resulted in *strong* character. But because many of the kids we came in contact with had successful but *uninvolved* fathers, I knew that I needed to be *warm* and *caring* as well.

I noticed that Jesus modeled *involvement* in the lives of people—that He trained and *released* His disciples to be all they were created to be by the Father. His example inspired me to take time with my wife and kids, to *listen* and to *have fun*.

Because we met so many young people who were searching for meaning in cults and Eastern religions, I saw how important it was to teach my kids to *think* biblically—or they, too, could get sucked into some false but appealing religious cult.

Most of all, I wanted to be the kind of man who *trusted* God, and lived out his *faith* in such a way that it inspired his wife and children to love God and trust Him for all their needs.

Sally and I didn't have kids for the first five years of our marriage, but we did talk a lot about our values. We made a decision early on that we were going to have breakfast every day with our kids, even though Sally didn't like breakfast and I was a loner in the mornings. Six months before our daughter Misha was born, Sally and I started having breakfast together so a habit would already be established when our firstborn made her entrance into the world. We made a minor lifestyle adjustment to fit a major value: to make *time* to be with our children.

I knew I was always going to live a very busy life, so I had to decide how I was going to handle my schedule and still be there for my kids. I made it a goal to come home right after work and spend two or three hours each evening with my children. I wanted to help them get ready for bed, to talk with them while Sally got the meal ready, to tell them stories. So that's what we did. I was busy four or five nights a week, but because I spent time with my kids the remaining nights, they always thought I was home; they didn't know any better until they were eight or nine years old.

My two children, Misha and Matthew, are 21 and 19 now, and we still have a great time together. We haven't always seen eye to eye and we've had to struggle through some difficult times, but we're a team. I don't know what the future holds, but I am sure of two things: first, that some serious challenges lie ahead for us; and second, that we'll meet them together. That's the only way a family can make it through the pressures of twentieth-century living—together. *Together* we're meeting this challenge called life and *together* we've hammered out the nonnegotiables that have enabled us to make it this far.

## WHAT ABOUT YOU?

Dads, I really must ask you a question. Do you know your own nonnegotiable values for life? You can't afford to be unsure; the world is far too hostile a place for that.

David Moore, pastor of Southwest Community Church in Palm Desert, California, uses a fascinating illustration to describe the plight of today's Christian fathers. David's dad used to bring home gifts when he returned from trips. Once he brought home a balsa-wood airplane with a plastic propeller wound up with a little rubber band. David says a lot of dads are like that airplane—huge expectations are placed on them and their rubber band gets wound tighter and tighter. It's no wonder that a lot of dads take flight or break! It's only the dads who are *sure* of the nonnegotiables in their life who will be able to stand up to the pressure.

In our society, especially in the Christian world, we often lift up women on Mother's Day. We honor them and give them flowers, and so we should. But while we *cherish* motherhood, we *demand* of fatherhood. I think men need appreciation and encouragement just as much as women. That's one reason I wrote this book: to encourage you and lift you up as much as I can.

I sure don't have all the answers, but I've stubbed my toes enough times; have been blessed with the friendships of many godly, wise fathers all across the world; and have gleaned some crucial truths from God's Word, all of which helps me be able to point in the right direction.

I really want you to succeed. In fact, I want it urgently. Fatherlessness is the most pressing need today in America, and I believe it will have the greatest negative impact on us and our children and our children's children. Like never before, we need good dads. My earnest prayer is that this book might help you move further down the road to becoming God's man in your family.

# The Nine Nonnegotiables:
# Caring for the Ones You Love

*God's man in the family
is committed to...*

1. Living a *godly* life by fearing the Lord

2. Developing *strong character*

3. Displaying *warmth and care*

4. Being *involved* in the lives of his wife and children

5. Becoming a good *listener*

6. Initiating *fun* in family life

7. Encouraging his children to *think* biblically

8. Living as one who *trusts* God completely

9. Living out his *faith* in a way that inspires his wife and children to develop a radical trust in God

# What's a Man to Do?

*Small boys learn to be large men in the presence*
*of large men who care about small boys.*

Life is full of "good news, bad news." I recently heard a true story about a young man in Portland, Oregon, who knows all about both. The bad news for him was that someone stole his motorcycle. The good news was that a year later he spotted his bike outside a tavern, took out a key he had kept in his wallet, started up his bike, and rode off. The bad news was that about 15 minutes later a policeman spotted him and pulled him over for failure to wear a helmet. The policeman checked the bike's registration and discovered it was stolen, then read him his rights and began to arrest him. The good news is the young man eventually proved to the police that the bike was his. At that point the police asked the young man if he would help them catch the thief, so they returned to the tavern (leaving the bike next door to be watched over by a service station attendant), surrounded the building, and waited for the thief to try to claim the bike. The bad news is that while they waited outside the tavern, the thief slipped through, walked over to the service station, and re-stole the bike! Unfortunately for the young man, that's where the story ends.

If we're honest, we have to admit that there is both good news and bad news about being a man in today's world. The good news is that Christian men are showing tremendous interest in becoming good fathers and dads. The bad news is that many men labor under tremendous pressures that far too often wilt their wills and wreck their resolve.

In a recent survey, 80 percent of the fathers interviewed said they would not want children if they could do it over again. I was amazed. Their response reflects the pressure on men to be good husbands, fathers, and friends.

So what is a man to do? How can we make sure we are God's man in the family? What can we do to ensure that our actions match our intentions? Maybe it would help to first scout out this "God's man" territory a little further.

## THE GOOD NEWS

A number of men's ministries have sprouted up all over the country during the last 10 or 15 years. Consider

*The Promise Keepers*, an organization that each summer attracts tens of thousands of men from across the nation to Colorado for a week of inspirational meetings focused on their roles as husbands and fathers. Or, think of the growing importance of family-oriented ministries such as *Focus on the Family* or Campus Crusade's *Family Ministry*. Or, take a look at the shelves of men's books that have crowded Christian bookstores in the last few years.

Good news can also be discovered in encouraging polls which consistently show that a high percentage of men are enjoying their marriages. We don't often hear about happy marriages in the secular press (or, for that matter, in the Christian press). We tend to say, "Look at all the problems! Gee, we're in bad shape."

Writer Andrew Greeley has done surveys all over the United States and has found that some 80 percent of currently married men are committed to fidelity.[1] Greeley concludes that people want to be happy in marriage and they want their marriages to work—it's just that staggering pressures tend to overwhelm them and they respond wrongly. I agree with Greeley. We men want to do a good job as husbands and dads.

## THE BAD NEWS

*Pressure*—that's the bad news. Men are facing unprecedented pressures today in our fast-paced world. Roles are confused and men are growing weary.

When people ask a father, "What are your children going to do for a living? What college are they going to? What kind of grades do they get?" they're judging not only his children, but him as well. This puts pressure on us dads to perform—to come up with the goods, so to speak.

> *Men have greater expecta-*
> *tions placed on them than*
> *ever before, but less time to*
> *fulfill them.*

Men also face growing *economic* pressures. They need a job and a half to keep up with the typical lifestyle of a middle-class American family. Ten years ago you could get along fine with one job; not anymore. Today you need 50 percent more money just to stay even.

Men face *time* pressures. Most men have to drive a long way to work. They come home tired and don't have the energy to be the good husbands and dads they are expected to be. They are expected to hold down at least one good job, attend church regularly, lead the home heroically, and even have some significant civic or community involvement on the side!

Men have greater expectations placed on them than ever before, but less time to fulfill them. Men know about kids in need, that divorce is destroying families, that kids are getting abused. They have heard that every minute or so in the United States, a teenager attempts to take his or her life.

I don't want to rub it in, but the grim reality is that 40 percent of the kids born between 1970 and 1984 do not spend their childhood with both parents. In 1960, 5 percent of kids lived with their moms only; in 1990, 25 percent were living with their moms only. Our society is undergoing tremendous change.

Dads who are divorced face the added pressure of a *failed marriage*. Guilt and a crushing sense of failure tend to haunt divorced men more strongly than other dads. And still, the pressure grows.

There are *role* pressures. Our world has changed radically since biblical times. Roles that the New Testament assumes—based on a stable, Jewish background—simply do not characterize the modern world. We live in a varied and culturally diverse society in which the role model of father is much less clear than it was for first-century dads. Are we Mr. Dad or Mr. Mom? Even the church is struggling to define the roles of men and women. How are we supposed to lead? Do we *tell* our wives what to do when we lead spiritually, or are we expected to be some kind of nurturing but tough, tender yet strong, shining and perfect example?

Many wives today have higher and higher expectations of their husbands. Unfortunately, they don't know when to be sure their man has pulled it off. How good a job must a man do for his wife to feel he has performed satisfactorily? Most men feel their wives want them to be a better parent, better husband, better lover, better communicator, and better emotionally; but they have a vague feeling their wives don't trust them to pull it off. After all, we lose our keys a lot, we get lost driving around town, and we're unwilling to stop at a gas station to ask for directions. The message comes through clearly: "You're probably not reliable—but you should be!"

Last, there are *spiritual* pressures. Many men believe they don't have the resources or the time to be spiritual, nor have they had the role models they needed. Few have had a close-up view of what a spiritual dad looked like.

These pressures make the father's role difficult. And if you are like me, you are afraid of failing, but don't have the time to succeed!

## SOCIETY TO THE ... RESCUE?

To fill these deep voids, society is trying to develop its own model of the ideal father, but its definitions seem neither clear nor helpful.

Ask the media what a father and a husband should be, and you'll get an earful. How about Tim the Toolman? Would you prefer Al Bundy? Or maybe Homer Simpson? Tune in to the talk shows, and you'll get yet other versions of the ideal dad. While the suggested role models change, one message comes through loud and clear: Dads, we need to be good all the time. Oprah and Phil are only too happy to tell us what great dads we should be.

But what does it mean to be a "great dad"? Does being a good father mean learning how to be a good mother? Modern psychologists cannot agree even among themselves on whether there is a significant difference between men and women (besides their "plumbing"). More and more, our culture takes pride in being egalitarian. Men today are expected to be tender, caring, and sensitive as well as strong, protecting, and providing.

In addition, many subtle, antifather messages come through some wings of the feminist movement. By demanding a false kind of equality, some have not only declared that male and female roles are the same, but that gender is the same. The result is a kind of neutered man, which some men have reacted against by trying to become hypermacho: They strip down to war paint, head out to the woods, and beat on drums.

This whole bewildering scene leads many men to despair. Nevertheless, they really do want to do what is right. Even though they live under explosive pressures and are daily forced to sift through a dizzying variety of conflicting signals, men honestly want to do what is right. In fact, they are committed to it.

They're just not sure what "it" is.

## A JOURNEY TO THE PAST

Every month, 299,800 men become fathers in the United States. The question is, how many of them succeed at being good fathers and dads?

If we fathers want to get our bearings—if we want to point ourselves in the direction of effective fatherhood—it's crucial that we consider how the New Testament defines our role. For although our culture is vastly different from the world of the ancient Near East, it is only in God's Word that we will find the compass points that can help us become the fathers we so desperately want to be.

Ancient Israel enjoyed a durable, agrarian, monocultural society that gave birth to a stable and well-defined role for parents. Mothers took the lead in rearing children until their kids had reached the age of four. Fathers were there as a provider, protector, and giver of stability and took center stage for the children's formation from the age of four onward.

Interestingly, this pattern is still the rule in the Middle East. Several years ago when we lived in Afghanistan, we saw mothers nurse their children until they reached three years of age. Mothers never let their children get out of eyesight and carried them wherever they went.

When a boy in Bible times turned four years old, the primary role model in his life switched. Mother had nurtured the child up until that time by supervising his care and upbringing. Now father took the lead and began his instruction. He was to do two basic things for his son: teach him the Torah, the Law of God (*see* Deuteronomy 6:4-9), and to teach him a trade.

Fathers were expected to fulfill these obligations in several ways. They were to help their sons memorize the Law, to understand the Law, and to engage their sons in questions as to how the Law applied practically.

While in Jerusalem at a conference recently, I watched a father doing exactly this with his son. It was wonderful. The two of them were walking down the street on the Sabbath. This father, sporting the long curls characteristic of orthodox Jews, plied his 12-or-so-year-old son with questions. They would laugh together and then the father would ask more questions in a very rabbinic sort of exercise. I was enthralled as I watched the Old Testament come to life right before my eyes. We don't see much of this father-son mentoring in our culture, but it was a norm in Bible times.

Every day a son joined his father for morning and evening prayers, and on the Sabbath they attended synagogue. When the son grew older, he was enrolled in the Sabbath school in the synagogue. So in ancient Jewish communities, informal instruction, formal schooling, and the spiritual life were all integrated.

But religious training comprised only half of a father's duty. Fathers also were expected to teach their sons a trade. Apprenticing took place right in the home. By age 15 a son was a full-time apprentice in his father's work. He worked side by side with his father, learning the secrets that would give him success when it was his turn to earn a living for his own family.

Perhaps the most famous example of this system is Jesus and Joseph. A fascinating passage in John 5:19 may well give us insight into how close a father drew to his son through this apprenticeship. In that passage, Jesus is speaking about His own relationship to the heavenly Father. He says, "I tell you the truth, the Son can do nothing by himself; he can do only what he sees his Father doing, because whatever the Father does the Son also does."

J.I. Packer suggests that Jesus was able to say this so forcefully because of the way Joseph had apprenticed Him. There is an overlap of meaning: just as Joseph apprenticed Jesus and showed Him all that he knew of carpentry, so the heavenly Father showed the Son exactly what He was to do. Joseph would have explained to Jesus how to make a piece of furniture, then he would have demonstrated it with his hands. Jesus would have learned by listening to His father, then by observing what His father did, then by imitating His father, then by doing it Himself with His father coaching on the sidelines. Jesus enjoyed an intimate and extensive association with His earthly father. In this way the Lord became a master craftsman through being modeled and guided by His father.

Such was the normal fathering role assumed in the New Testament. A son not only learned a trade from his father, he learned how to work with people, how to manage money, how to plan, how to be a responsible provider. He learned at his father's side, whether his dad was a carpenter or a farmer or a fisherman.

## THE SCENE CHANGES

This family pattern continued for many centuries, but the picture changed radically with the advent of the Industrial Revolution. The family went from being a unit of production (where work and family were integrated) to a unit of consumption. New values replaced time-honored ones. For example, while financial independence is highly desirable to us, it is foreign to the New Testament. Today we expect to gain independence from our families, to grow away from them, and to get our own place and our own identity. But those thoughts never would have occurred to a son in Bible times.

Separating work and family opened the way to a whole new set of unbiblical values. No longer were men an integral part of the domestic sphere. Men started to become strangers in their own homes.

According to one expert,[2] until about 1830, all child-rearing manuals were addressed to men; but with the dawning of the Industrial Revolution, such books turned their attention to women. It made perfect sense. Fathers were being forced out of the home to go away to work, and mothers became the dominant influence in the home.

These cataclysmic social changes have led to the phenomenon of the disappearing dad and have turned fatherhood into a Sunday institution. Whether we like it or not, fathers have been sidelined in our modern culture. *The challenge for us as men is to go back and identify a set of nonnegotiable values* that will give us the strength to counter a culture and a world that is unbiblical in its very foundation and structures. We need to take back the role of provider and spiritual discipler—a role that has been taken from us.

> *If we want to succeed as husbands and fathers, we must know what the "non-negotiables" are.*

The sad truth is, we are being compromised without choosing to be compromised. Men today suffer tremendous stress trying to balance work, home, and church. If we want to succeed as husbands and fathers—and if you are reading this book, I know you do want to be God's man in the family—we must know what the "nonnegotiables" are. That's the only way we will be able to become who God created us to be.

## SEARCHING FOR IMPACT MAKERS

I'd like to close this chapter with a question. Please, pause a few moments to ponder your response before you read on. Here's the question: What men have made the greatest impact on your life?

You may be thinking of your father, an uncle, a grandfather, mentors, brothers, teachers, pastors, coaches, or neighbors. What was it about them that made such an impact on you?

Once you have these men in mind, I'd like you to list ten characteristics that describe their influence on you. Were they fun-loving? Accepting? Adventurous? Smart? What was it that made them pop into your mind? Write out your answers here:

1. _____

2. _____

3. _____

4. _____

5. _____

6. _____

7. _____

8. _____

9. _____

10. _____

After you have completed your list, look at the words you wrote and ask yourself one more question: "What kind of man would I like to be so that someday boys or girls—my kids and others—would say, 'I want to be like him'?" In fact, after you reflect on that question, why don't you write the list again, only this time make it more personal. List ten principles you want to live by that are worth dying for—that you won't give up for anything or anyone. Write them here:

1. _____

2. _____

3. _____

4. _____

5. _____

6. _____

7. _____

8. _____

9. _____

10. _____

With this list in mind, you're well on your way to discovering your own nonnegotiables in this challenging but rewarding business of fatherhood.

## ACTION STEPS

- In ancient Israel, fathers were very much involved in the spiritual upbringing of their sons, and this is an excellent principle worthy of imitating with our children today. Have your children pick out a Bible-story book they would like to read with you, and use the story time as an opportunity to share an important Bible truth or lesson with them.

- Look at your second list of ten answers on page 31— answers to the question, "What kind of man would I like to be?" Select and do one item on the list that you would like to put into action with your family *today*. Take the other nine items, and decide how you can fulfill them in the next week or two, and place a checkmark by them as you do so. After you are done, go through the list again, and continue putting these items into action...let them become part and parcel of your life.

# 2

# Learning to Be God's Man

"The fear of the LORD is the beginning of wisdom," says Proverbs 9:10. I'm convinced it's also the beginning of being God's man.

I first began to make this discovery when I started junior high school. Every evening I walked home by a drugstore. In that store was a rack of magazines, and on that rack was a porno shelf with two to three examples of the type we are all too familiar with. My friends were in the habit of going into that store and salivating over those magazines. I admit there were times when I joined them...but it was terrible on my nerves. Guilt and worry bothered me, but not nearly so much as a deeper struggle going on in my heart. My real dilemma was this: What would my actions do to my dad if he found out? Try as I might, I couldn't shake the awful thought that *what I'm doing will cut him to the heart.*

You see, my dad feared the Lord, and that conviction had a profound effect on my life. But to see just how profound, we need to back up a bit.

## A MAN WHO FEARED THE LORD

In our fundamentalist church you could find every level of spiritual maturity. There were godly, prayer-warrior types sitting right next to some real weirdos—the good, the bad, and the ugly, you might say. I couldn't help but look around that church and think, *I don't want anything to do with this.*

And yet one thing pulled at me constantly. My mom and dad remained there like rocks. They were so real and so godly and so mature and so genuine that you couldn't deny the reality of their faith.

Dad came across the States in a classic *Grapes of Wrath* kind of story. In 1934 his parents loaded up their nine kids in the family Model T and took two-and-half months to travel the dusty roads from Oklahoma to California. They camped out along the way, following the fruit and vegetable harvests up and down the West Coast. They picked cotton in Arizona, apples in Washington. They worked in the Imperial Valley in Southern California and in the San Joaquin Valley of Central California. When he was 18 my dad got saved in a little Assembly of God church in Tulare, California.

He traces his family heritage back to four Irish brothers who sailed across the Atlantic in the 1740s. We McClungs boast a long line of thieves and preachers in our lineage (once upon a time the distinction was a little clearer than it is today). Our family genealogy features name after name of Baptist and Presbyterian pastors and preachers. We're blessed with a wonderful heritage.

My mom and dad got married when they were both very young, and at 21 my dad was picked out by the elders of the little church he was attending to fill in for the pastor, who had died suddenly of a heart attack. The elders intended for him to fill in only as long as it took to find another pastor, but once he got behind a pulpit he never left. He moved to Arizona to pastor a church, finished high school while pastoring, then went to Bible college. To this day he lives with the awareness that his education is not nearly as thorough as that of many of the men in the churches he has pastored.

Despite his lack of impressive academic credentials, in 1967 he was invited to pioneer a church for seminary professors and church officials who were dissatisfied with the emotional excesses that plagued some churches in the denomination. These men wanted more substance and they chose dad as their pastor because he had a reputation as a godly man. So he became the spiritual leader of a church that eventually grew to about 1,000 people, including 75-100 members with earned masters and doctoral degrees.

My dad is a pastor's pastor. He has made a career out of taking split churches and putting them back together or planting new ones. My earliest memories are of him planting a storefront church in Long Beach, California. I can remember evangelists coming through and the people crowding in on little benches. Dad would go out into the streets and invite folks in. He built the church in Long Beach into a fine congregation, then left to do the same thing in another city.

Many, many mornings I would wake up for school and hear my dad praying in his bedroom. Some afternoons I would see him go to the church. That night I would ask mom, "Where's Dad?" and she would say, "He is in the church, praying." Or I would get up the next morning and ask, "Where's Dad?" and get the same reply. Dad would often spend the whole night at the church, praying. That's just my dad—he set a wonderful example for all of us.

---

*He was a heart man who*
*practiced heart religion.*

---

Dad was what I call "a heart preacher." Our denomination came out of the Wesleyan Methodist holiness tradition and sometimes it got stuck in legalism. Dad acknowledged the rules and he upheld them, but the rules weren't *him*. When we kids became teenagers, we attacked those rules passionately...and he threw them out, one at a time. We would say, "Dad, where does it say this in Scripture?" and if it wasn't there, the rule got the boot.

I still recall our long discussions. "Why is it wrong to go to movies if you can watch them on television?" I demanded. "Why don't you just teach us to discern between right and wrong?" Dad listened and considered, and despite the convictions of many in his denomination, he threw out the man-made rules. He was a heart man who practiced heart religion.

Dad never was a hellfire-and-brimstone preacher, but he feared God and he was not afraid to administer a little righteous anger when the situation called for it. I used to joke that on the back door of our house hung a belt with a sign over it that read, "I need thee every hour."

I was raised on the knee of a godly mother and across the knee of a godly father! Dad disciplined us. He was strict, but loving. When I tried to get away with something and mom caught me, she would say the line every child hates and fears: "Go to your bedroom and wait until your father gets home." I had gotten into the habit of putting a *Life* magazine underneath my Levis, which was great for about the first two or three spankings. It was not so great after my dad caught on!

Dad's whole ministry, and indeed all of his life, was full of the fruit of the Spirit. *Character* was the stamp on his ministry.

So when you consider that brief background, perhaps you can see what so deeply troubled me as I stood at that magazine rack, tempted to thumb through a pornographic magazine on my way home from school. I never once thought my dad would reject me, but I definitely feared how he would react to my oglings. No matter where he was physically, I knew that looking over my shoulder was this godly, righteous, Spirit-filled man whom I loved and admired deeply. It made me tremble to think how my sin would grieve him.

## FEAR AND FRIENDSHIP

The fear of the Lord shaped and molded every step

my dad took. He was not frightened of God, but he feared Him (a little more on that later). My dad drank deeply from the stream that lies hidden from so many today—he was close to God, and it was the fear of the Lord that drew the two of them together. He was a friend of God and he talked to his Friend all the time. Over the years it became a family joke. I have probably caught my dad mumbling to the Lord over 500 times in my life. We would be driving along and in a moment of quietness we would hear this low muttering. "There's dad praying again!" we would giggle. We kid him and tease him about it today, but we wouldn't change him for the world.

As a youngster, I often heard dad in the study or in the bedroom or found him in the living room talking to God with a profound sense of compassion. I frequently caught him praying and weeping for parishioners or church families by name, pouring out their problems and lifting them up to the Lord.

He exemplified Psalm 25:14 to me: "The friendship of the LORD is for those who fear him" (RSV). He had a rich friendship with God. He shared God's burdens and he shared his burdens with God. There's a closeness and intimacy with God that comes when we take His side.

## WHAT IS THE FEAR OF THE LORD?

If you have a hard time identifying with my dad's normal experience, unfortunately I would have to say you are not alone. I realize much of this is foreign to many believers today. We rarely hear sermons about the fear of the Lord, and if we do, we usually connect them with words such as "judgment" or "anger" or "condemning" or "severe."

And to be honest, the fear of the Lord *is* connected with those concepts. *But that is far from the whole story!* If the fear of the Lord was exclusively or even primarily a negative experience, Psalm 25:14 would make no sense. But there it is, standing tall and majestic in the midst of a tender poem about God's deep concern and care for His beloved people: "The friendship of the LORD is for those who fear him."

I said at the beginning of this chapter that the fear of the Lord is the beginning of being God's man, and I've illustrated my conviction with the best example I know of: my dad's life. But what does it mean exactly to "fear the Lord"? And how does fearing God supply the foundation for dads who want to provide their children with a loving, stable home?

For many people, "fear" and "love" don't go together any more than "fear" and "friendship" seem to. The people we fear we usually want to run away from, but we long to draw close to the people we love. Can you imagine anyone saying, "I really like Hank; he is my best friend, but I'm afraid to be around him"?

I can't imagine it, either. But I think that's where we make a huge mistake when it comes to the fear of the Lord. We imagine it means "to be afraid of," but it doesn't. A fear of God and being afraid of God are two separate things; otherwise, Moses' words to the Israelites make no sense: "Do *not be afraid*. God has come to test you, so that *the fear of God* will be with you to keep you from sinning" (Exodus 20:20, emphasis added).

"Don't be afraid," Moses said, "but instead, fear God." Moses saw the fear of God in a positive light. He saw it as a force that would keep the people from sinning and keep their fellowship with God strong and vibrant and real and even thrilling.

But what is the fear of the Lord? So many people today want to confine the idea to awe or respect, but I'm convinced that doesn't go quite far enough. Such people are usually eager to keep believers from becoming afraid of God, and I'm eager to do that as well. But there *is* an element of real fear in the fear of the Lord— knee-knocking, trembling, shaking, honest-to-goodness, breath-swallowing *fear*. And the reason is that God is God and we're not.

Have you ever stood on the edge of a vast precipice, such as the rim of the Grand Canyon, and looked down? The view was spectacular and the awesome sight took away your breath, but I would be willing to bet your experience was also tinged with some fear. Why? Because you knew that if you were to get on the "wrong side" of the precipice, so to speak, you would be dead in seconds. The vast distance between the canyon's rim and its floor has the power to kill you!

The fear of the Lord is something like that. If through faith in the risen Christ you have entrusted your soul to God's care, you have no need to be afraid of God. His judgment against sin has already been poured out on His sinless Son at Calvary. Still, because you are finite and small and fragile and God is infinite and everywhere and almighty, not everything in the feeling called fear vanishes when we come to know the Lord— just the life-threatening part.

> *Only those fathers who fear
> God will be able to lead
> their children into a rich,
> fulfilling, and lasting rela-
> tionship with the King of
> the universe.*

On a number of occasions I have been to the top of fantastically high, glass-enclosed office buildings. When I look down, even though I know it is impossible for me to fall through the safety glass to my death far below, the sheer awesomeness of the sight still puts fear into my heart. But it is a thrilling kind of fear that makes me appreciate life all the more.

The fear of the Lord can cause you to feel the same way. When you come to know God for who He is, an all-powerful, sovereign, awe-inspiring Lord who with a single command calls into being a universe of blazing stars, you will come to "delight in the fear of the LORD," even as did the Messiah Himself (*see* Isaiah 11:3).

Only those fathers who know God in this way, who fear Him with a holy and trembling fear, will be able to lead their children into a rich, fulfilling, and lasting relationship with the King of the universe. Only those fathers who see themselves for who they are and who honor God for who He is are capable of launching out boldly into life, confident that their awesome Lord is walking with them every step of the way.

## THE BENEFITS OF FEARING GOD

I do not see how men can afford to neglect developing a healthy fear of God in both themselves and in their families. And I mean "afford" in the strictest sense. Who would want to do without the following benefits promised to those who fear the Lord?

*Family well-being:* "Oh, that their hearts would be inclined to fear me and keep all my commands always, so that it might go well with them and their children forever!" (Deuteronomy 5:29).

*Protection:* "The angel of the LORD encamps around those who fear him, and he delivers them" (Psalm 34:7).

*Provision:* "Fear the LORD, you his saints, for those who fear him lack nothing" (Psalm 34:9).

*Food:* "He provides food for those who fear him; he remembers his covenant forever" (Psalm 111:5).

*Success:* "He sought God during the days of Zechariah, who instructed him in the fear of God. As long as he sought the LORD, God gave him success" (2 Chronicles 26:5).

*Fulfilled desires:* "He fulfills the desires of those who fear him; he hears their cry and saves them" (Psalm 145:19).

*God's goodness:* "How great is your goodness, which you have stored up for those who fear you, which you bestow in the sight of men on those who take refuge in you" (Psalm 31:19).

I could cite many more such promises, but you get the idea. The fear of the Lord is not some stuffy, out-dated, theological concept best hidden in the footnotes of a seminary textbook, but is an untamed, swelling river of life for anyone willing and adventurous enough to shoot its rapids.

My dad is one believer who every morning eagerly clambers into his raft of faith to shoot God's rapids. His healthy fear of the Lord brought about several note-worthy characteristics in his life, traits worth emulating by any Christian dad. Let's look at several of them.

1. *Because dad feared the Lord, pleasing God was his greatest aim.* He refused to get caught up in the politics of the church, even though he was in the center of the polit-ical life of our denomination. He would not preach any-thing extraneous to the gospel. He constantly preached about forgiveness, bitterness, love, jealousy, covetous-ness, and mercy. He made pleasing God the central aim of his life, and he lived out that commitment every day.

2. *Because dad feared the Lord, he believed that God judged sin—and he was not afraid to follow the Almighty's example with his children!* Dad lived by the conviction that there were consequences to sin and he enforced discipline in the home, but not in a mean or harsh man-ner.

The worst offense any of us children could commit was to disrespect mom. A couple times I lipped off to her and she covered me. But if dad ever found out, he would discipline me. He wasn't nasty, but he simply would not tolerate disrespect.

43

My dad indelibly impressed those lessons upon me. Years later when my own family lived in the red-light district of Amsterdam, ministering to the prostitutes and pimps of the city with a team from YWAM, I found myself calling upon dad's method of discipline. My daughter Misha was 13 or 14 years old and was growing more and more sassy toward Sally. She was nice to me, but would rip Sally apart when I was away from home.

One day I sat down with my daughter and said, "If you live in my house, you will respect your mom, not just as your mother, but as *my wife*. And if you don't, you may not live in this house. It's that serious. You make your choice. If you live and stay here, you will respect her. You may not agree with her; you may not think she's perfect. That's OK. But you will show respect for her. Otherwise, I won't let you stay. Things have to change. Period."

I learned such tough love from my dad. He meant what he said and he enforced it. I had confidence that my confrontation with Misha would turn out all right because that was how my dad related to me. Discipline is never easy to administer, but it will never grow overly harsh or unduly lenient if a healthy fear of the Lord controls you.

3. *Because my dad feared the Lord, he hated sin.* Dad was ashamed to speak about certain things, yet he was not prudish. I remember his eyes flashing at blatant sin, yet the dominant tone of his communication about that sin was always grief and brokenness. Through his reaction I was given insight into the heart of God.

I believe my dad's response to sin reflects God's heart. I think of the brokenness of God in Genesis 6:5,6:

"The LORD saw how great man's wickedness on the earth had become, and that every inclination of the thoughts of his heart was only evil all the time. The LORD was grieved that he had made man on the earth, and his heart was filled with pain." Or, I imagine the anger of God when Moses came down the mountain after receiving the Ten Commandments: "'I have seen these people,' the LORD said to Moses, 'and they are a stiff-necked people. Now leave me alone so that my anger may burn against them and that I may destroy them'" (Exodus 32:9,10). Texts like those have helped to shape my understanding of the fear of God and have given me a firm foundation for raising my family.

I have consciously tried to help my kids get to this point in their own lives. We were worried that as they were growing up in the red-light district, they would take sin for granted. After all, it surrounded them and they grew up with it. I was afraid sin wouldn't shock them like I thought it should.

We moved into the neighborhood when Matthew and Misha were three and five. By the time they reached 12 and 14, the sin around us seemed "normal" to them. It was just life. I became very concerned, especially when they became teenagers and began to express spiteful attitudes, a lack of respect, and a lack of seriousness about God.

That's what prompted me late one night to take each of them for a walk through the red-light district. "Look what you see," I told them. Misha and I were standing on a bridge in the worst part of the neighborhood when I said, "Listen! Look! I just want you to look at what you have seen for a long time, but have become calloused to; what's going on?"

As you scanned the pathetic figures hunching in the darkness, you would see drug addicts shooting up, others selling drugs, still others fighting. If you simply stood and observed for a while, you would see strife, tension, greed, mocking. It was a powerful moment. I said, "Mish, this is not nice, is it? This is sin. This is what sin does to people."

After midnight the area really unwound—unraveled is a better word. The shops and businesses had shut down by that time and the people started getting extremely aggressive. I took Matthew and Misha into that vile environment to make an impact on them. We walked through the neighborhood so they could be impressed with sin in the right sense, to witness firsthand what it does to people. Sin destroys people, it deceives them, it decimates their lives.

My dad taught me that "to fear the LORD is to hate evil" (Proverbs 8:13). To fear God is to see sin the way He sees it. It is to take God's side against sin. We must never side with a sinner who is angry at God, who is defending himself, who is deceived. And yet, because God is merciful, this doesn't produce a dilemma for us. We don't have to choose between hating sin and hating the sinner. We can love people but we can hate the evil, and we can hate it in them.

The fear of God eliminates a wrong kind of sympathy, a compromising, mushy approach to sin. The fear of God produces in us an abhorrence of evil. Suppose we went into a five-star, elegant restaurant and the waiter came out with a shovel full of stinking, steaming, fresh manure and dumped it on the table! We would react with abhorrence, and so we should. Why, then, don't we react to sin like that? Why is it that so often when we see sin, our first response is not loathing, but something more along the lines of, "Gee, that's too bad"? Men who want to be godly and who fear the Lord will abhor sin and see it for what it is.

Someone told me the other day about a man who had been involved in a string of illicit relationships. "I really think there's hope for him," the person told me. "His counselor said it's an addiction and that he can get over it in a matter of weeks."

I was grieved because I considered his response far too superficial. I believe wholeheartedly in restoration, but it cannot come before genuine repentance, and that sometimes takes a long time. A few days ago I received a call from an acquaintance about this man and he asked, "What is your advice? This man has an invitation to speak in a large evangelical church in the Midwest six months from now, and he doesn't know what to do." I replied, "It's very simple. He doesn't even think about going. What kind of statement would he be making about his problem if he followed your encouragement to take this engagement?"

"Well, right now we're just saying he is going through a very difficult time. We don't want to embarrass him and he has repented of his sin."

After that phone conversation, I was grieved. I wondered why this person was being protected from the natural consequences of his sin—shame, embarrassment, grief. Those are some of the means God uses to train us to steer clear of sin. My dad taught me that those who fear God are aware of the consequences of sin and do not try to cut off the process of consequences that God uses to discipline those He loves.

4. *Because my dad feared the Lord, he was a humble man.* Humility marked my dad's life. He was a teachable man. You could approach him. Although he was godly and there was a certain soberness about him, we could talk to him. He didn't give us platitudes, and we appreciated him for that.

At the heart of humility is honesty. Knowing who you really are and admitting it honestly is humility. Pride can only develop in the heart of someone who refuses to be honest with himself. A proud person overestimates his own abilities and achievements and minimizes those of others, and at the same time downplays his weaknesses and failures and magnifies the foibles of others. In contrast, a humble person is an honest, transparent person.

The Holy Spirit loves honesty in us and in other people. We all instinctively trust people who will humble themselves and admit their need or their mistakes. If they abuse that trust, obviously the trust evaporates. But if they blow it once or twice and humble themselves and deal with it, we trust them. We'll forgive even a president if he is honest and straightforward with us. That's why Richard Nixon has been so vilified as a political figure: We don't trust people who have problems but try to hide them.

Humility allows us to go to God and draw from Him. We can say, "God, I have a weakness in this area and I know You have the answers, so I'm coming to You to meet my need." If as men we know how to be honest with God about our weaknesses and our needs and trust Him to meet those needs, we will better know how to deal with a problem brought to us by our wife or kids. Even if we don't know how to respond, we can say, "Well,

I don't have the answer, but let's go to the Lord. Let's ask Him for wisdom; let's ask Him for strength and encouragement." And because we're humble (that is, honest), we become an example to them.

My kids don't expect me to have all the answers, but they do want me to be honest with them and to point them to God and to go *with* them to God. The fear of the Lord doesn't produce an untouchable level of super-righteousness. It produces a kind of holiness that's approachable, a kind of righteousness that's inspiring and motivating. It makes us like Jesus. He motivates us because He is so real and caring and yet so righteous and holy. A true and healthy fear of the Lord does all this for us.

## CHOOSING THE FEAR OF THE LORD

No one fears the Lord because it is in his genes. No one fears God because his parents did. My dad *chose* to fear God. He had an opportunity, over and over again, to involve himself in the wrong kind of religion, in legalism, and party politics. But he refused to do it. *He chose the fear of the Lord.*

It was only later that I discovered this nonnegotiable principle in Scripture in Proverbs 1:29. That verse states that we must *choose* to fear the Lord. But to get the full flavor of the verse, you have to read the preceding verses as well. Wisdom is speaking, and says:

> Since you ignored all my advice
>   and would not accept my rebuke,
> I in turn will laugh at your disaster;
>   I will mock when calamity overtakes you—

> when calamity overtakes you like a storm,
>     when disaster sweeps over you like a whirl-
>     wind, when distress and troubles overwhelm
>     you.
>
> Then they will call to me but I will not answer;
>     they will look for me but will not find me.
>
> Since they hated knowledge
>     *and did not choose to fear the LORD,*
>
> since they would not accept my advice
>     and spurned my rebuke,
>
> they will eat the fruit of their ways
>     and be filled with the fruit of their schemes.
>
> —*Proverbs 1:25-31, emphasis added*

All the disasters described in this passage came upon the Israelites for just one reason: They did not choose the fear of the Lord.

Fear of God in the biblical sense doesn't just happen to a person. My dad chose it, and I have decided to follow his example. Years ago I realized, *I can choose this. The fear of the Lord won't appear in my life just because it happened to my dad.* I had to choose it just as he did *...and so do you.*

Let's stop right here for a moment. I want to ask you to do what my dad did, and what I have chosen to do. I ask you to choose to fear God. I don't know how to make it any more simple than that. Just kneel or bow your head, and pray to God, humble yourself before Him as a holy God, and tell Him you choose to fear Him. Ask Him to put the fear of the Lord in your heart. Tell Him you choose to love what He loves and to hate what

He hates. Receive the fear of God by faith in your heart. And choose the fear of the Lord every day of your life from now on. Of course, we need to make the same choice when we face the temptation to sin. That shows we are serious about fearing God.

## WANTED: GODLY MEN

The fear of God produces godliness. Now, godliness is not something that happens to us like magic, instantly, overnight. It is developed in our lives over time through the work of the Holy Spirit—by hating sin, by loving what God loves, by seeking to be close to God, and by asking ourselves, "Does this thing I want to do grieve God or does it make Him happy?"

The two values at the forefront of most American minds are *happiness* and *freedom*. Those values dominate every other issue. That's why the pro-life movement is so offensive to our society: It challenges people's "right" to be "happy" and "free" in the way they want to live.

The fear of the Lord says, "My first goal in life is not to seek what is going to make me happy, but what is going to make God happy. Is this going to please Him, delight Him, bring joy to Him? I believe that if it does that to Him, it will do that for me."

I've talked a lot about my dad in this chapter and about how the fear of God shaped and molded his life. It should be obvious that my dad is a spiritual hero for me, but it is also important for you to know he wasn't perfect. He had a short temper. Oh, he never screamed or yelled or threw things, but at times he was irritable and impatient.

Once some time ago my dad was leading a tour of church people through Europe and two of the ladies were consistently late. One day my dad was pacing outside of the bus and my mom was trying to encourage him to "be careful, be nice, be patient." The "patient" word punched his button. He spit out, "I've got more patience than you give me credit for!" Mom delights in telling this story and we all laugh about his shortness of temper.

Nevertheless, dad is a hero for me.

I've asked myself, Why is he a hero? I should point out that a hero differs from a celebrity. A celebrity is famous, and my dad is not famous. A hero is someone to look up to in the way he lives, how he deals with problems, and how faithful he has been to God and righteousness and truth. Also, when a hero makes a mistake, he is not afraid to admit it.

---

*If we want to become heroes to our kids, the key is that we learn to fear the Lord.*

---

We need spiritual heroes today, and the fear of God is what produces them. This is what makes a dad a spiritual hero to his kids. They will forgive a lot of sins if a dad is honest, if he is real, if he is involved with them. They want him to be a hero and they want him to succeed, even more than he wants it. So as dads, we don't need to worry too much about our failures and our weaknesses if we're being honest with our kids, if we're dealing with them righteously, if we're taking God's side against sin, and *if we're being accountable.*

That's what will make us heroes to our kids. We don't need a cape and we don't need a mask or a telephone booth or a bat cave or even a sidekick. If we want to become heroes to our kids, the key is that we learn to fear the Lord.

And God help us if we don't.

## MISERABLE IS THE FAMILY THAT DOESN'T FEAR GOD

There are only a few texts in the New Testament that deal directly with family issues, and Romans 3:10-18 isn't one of them. Yet I believe this passage goes a long way toward explaining what is happening to families across America, even Christian families.

In nine short verses, the apostle Paul quotes no fewer than eight Old Testament passages. He does it in machine-gun fashion, quick and deadly. His purpose is to picture in sharp but unflattering terms the rebellion of men and women, boys and girls, all across the globe. Read for yourself his gruesome portrait:

> As it is written:
>
> "There is no one righteous, not even one;
>     there is no one who understands,
>     no one who seeks God.
>
> All have turned away,
>     they have together become worthless;

there is no one who does good,
not even one."

"Their throats are open graves;
their tongues practice deceit."

"The poison of vipers is on their lips."
"Their mouths are full of cursing and bitterness."

"Their feet are swift to shed blood;
ruin and misery mark their ways,

and the way of peace they do not know."
*"There is no fear of God before their eyes."*
*—Romans 3:10-18, emphasis added*

Notice carefully how the apostle sums up this foul list of degrading sins: "There is no fear of God before their eyes." Every vile activity, every murderous intention, every lying word described in his collection of verses could be traced to one single cause: *There is no fear of God before their eyes.*

It's a passage like this that convinces me I am right when I say that the fear of the Lord is the beginning of being God's man. Do you want to see a picture of a home that doesn't operate under the fear of God? You have a ghastly one in Romans 3:10-18. It's a home which:

- fails to understand God
- fails to seek God
- is unconcerned about the needs of others
- does no good

- is filled with lying and deceit
- brings pain and hurt to others
- is foulmouthed
- is consumed with bitterness
- easily descends into violence and anger
- is headed for ruin and misery
- lacks peace and unity

What kind of emotional and spiritual atmosphere were you raised in? What kind prevails in your home right now? Please take a moment to describe the spiritual climate you grew up in and the atmosphere that exists in your family right now: Peaceful or full of conflict? Harsh or kind words spoken? Truthful or lying? Angry or gentle? God-fearing or ungodly? Respectful or demeaning? Jealous or generous? Fun-loving or sad? Abusive or loving? Encouraging or mocking? and so on.

_____    _____

_____    _____

_____    _____

_____    _____

If the atmosphere is not what it should be, *it can change*. That is God's promise to those who fear Him. It will take time, and it must involve your choices, but if you lead your family in the fear of God, your home will change! You can begin a new way of life and create a new heritage for your family. You must choose.

Do you want a home like the one described in Romans

3:10-18? Or would you rather have a family blessed by the fear of God? Many American families are perched on a track headed for destruction. They have climbed aboard, the train is leaving the station, the engine is straining at full power, and before you know it, they will have arrived at their destination: "ruin and misery mark their ways" (Romans 3:16).

It's not a pretty sight. *But it doesn't have to be that way at all!* Anyone can get off this train to catastrophe any time he wants to. All he needs is a ticket.

You may not have realized it, but this train works differently than most. Everybody on the face of the planet is on board. All of us have chosen to ride the rails. But we don't have to stay there. If we want to get off and avoid ending up where we don't want to go, all we need is the ticket marked, "The fear of the Lord."

The fear of God produces in a family righteousness, hunger for God, unselfishness, honesty, blessings, unity, peace, and healing. What man wouldn't love to have those things busting out all over in his home? Choosing to fear the Lord helps to direct our actions, reactions, and motivations toward pleasing God and becoming like the Lord Jesus.

Men, the fear of the Lord is the beginning of good fatherhood. It is the basis of everything else. In fact, if that is your choice, I urge you to go back and read this chapter again, but this time, do it on your knees, prayerfully.

If you want your family to stay off the train, I'd advise you to visit the heavenly Ticket Counter...quickly, before your caboose comes to rest in a ghost town called Ruin.

# _____ ACTION STEPS _____

- Psalm 25:14 says, "The friendship of the LORD is for those who fear him" (RSV). How would you rate your friendship with the Lord right now? What one change can you make in your life now to draw closer to Him?

- A man who fears the Lord will make pleasing God his greatest aim. One person got a small tablet of yellow Post-It note paper and wrote, "Will this please God?" on each paper and attached one to the TV, another to the steering wheel of his car, and yet another on the refrigerator! Perhaps you won't want to do that, but it *is* a good idea to habitually ask yourself, "What can I do that will please the Lord today?" In fact, think of something you can do right now, and put your thought into action!

- A celebrity is famous, and a hero is someone you can look up to. One way to become a hero is through more involvement with your kids. Plan a block of time—at least one or two hours—to spend together with your kids, and let *them* choose the activity . . . perhaps riding bicycles, visiting a park, drawing pictures, reading a book, or playing an outdoor game. Get involved and enjoy yourself!

# Taking Back What Is Yours

I know a pastor in Florida whose daughter was dating a deacon's son. She was 17, a great kid, and father and daughter had always enjoyed a great friendship. But their relationship began to sour when she started dating this young man. He had an arrogant attitude, and she started adopting his disposition.

One night the young man came to see the young lady and my pastor friend met him on the front yard to tell him he could never see her again. "In fact," this pastor said, "I told him that if he tried to see her again, I would fight him physically. I would do whatever it took to keep him away. I felt as if God had said to me that I was going to lose my daughter to an unrighteous kid, and that she was worth fighting for."

Early the next day the young man's father, the deacon, called the pastor and ripped into him. My friend replied, "The reason your son has so many problems is that you're not right with God. I don't care what you think of me. You get your life right and your son will be OK, and then you will appreciate me. But even if you don't, that's OK with me. I did what I had to do."

My friend's daughter would not speak to her dad for two weeks. Nevertheless, he kept making himself available to her and reaching out to her and trying to express his heart. One day he went into her room to sit down and talk with her. "Can I just tell you why I did this?" he asked. She let him speak to her for the first time in weeks, and at the end of their conversation, she broke. She threw her arms around her father and said, "Thank you, dad. I needed you to do that. I was so proud that you had done it in that way. Thank you, dad, you did the right thing. You saved me."

In risking his daughter's anger, that pastor displayed real strength—the kind of strength that keeps families together and growing in their walk with God. When I talk about strength in this chapter, I'm not talking about the Marlboro man or the Terminator. I'm not talking about big biceps or taking steroids. Those things don't describe or produce courage, the kind of strength men need in today's world.

## GETTING TOUGH GOD'S WAY

Real strength comes from being godly, from fearing God. I know that sounds contradictory, but it's true. Normally we think that fear is a sign of weakness. But in God's kingdom, fearing God is precisely what gives a man strength and prevents him from fearing mere men.

Proverbs 29:25 says that "fear of man will prove to be a snare." So how do we avoid the "snare"? Isaiah tells us: "Do not fear what they fear, and do not dread it. The LORD Almighty is the one you are to regard as holy, he is the one you are to fear" (Isaiah 8:12,13).

What dads need today, perhaps more than ever, is the kind of strength that gives us the fortitude to say no. It is important to be able to say no to being a couch potato when we come home from work tired. It is important to be able to say no to overspending and getting in debt. It is important to be able to say no when our kids try to take over the spiritual atmosphere of our home. It is important to say no to the temptation to turn off our mind and stop learning and thinking.

The fear of God gives us the courage and strength to stand up to dirty jokes, R-rated movies, and compromise at work. Being strong in the Lord Jesus frees us from bowing down to the expectations of others and from caving in to their continual demands to do what they want us to do regardless of the effect on our family.

From a human perspective, the early church had plenty of reason to be afraid. Some of their people were beaten, others were tossed in jail, still others were executed. Life was not easy for a follower of Jesus in those days! Yet the church's numbers exploded. Why? The book of Acts tells us: "Then the church throughout Judea, Galilee and Samaria...was strengthened; and encouraged by the Holy Spirit, it grew in numbers, living in the fear of the Lord" (Acts 9:31).

It is no accident that the phrases "grew in numbers" and "was strengthened" are found right next to "living in the fear of the Lord." That's what living in the fear of the Lord always does: it causes growth and gives strength, both in a church and in our families.

## WHAT IS GODLY STRENGTH?

Joshua is one of the best examples of a man who needed godly strength if he was to succeed. God told Joshua to be strong and courageous no less than *four times* by the end of the first chapter of his book (*see* verses 6,7,9,18). Obviously, Joshua *needed* to be encouraged to be strong and courageous! And that's really not so tough to understand. If I had been Moses' assistant and I were getting ready to lead nearly two million stubborn people into a strange new homeland, I'm sure I would need God to tell me to be strong!

What did it mean for Joshua to be strong and courageous? What does that mean for you? There are at least five elements of strength Joshua needed to become God's man.

1. *Joshua needed to claim what was his.* He had an inheritance for himself. God had promised him, "I will give you every place where you set your foot" (Joshua 1:3). He had a leadership role to take and he needed to take hold of it and not allow it to pass him by. The success of the nation would turn largely on his willingness and ability to lead with strength and conviction.

Joshua's one notable failure is also connected to the one instance when he failed to be strong and courageous. Joshua 7 details the sin of Achan, who kept for himself some of the spoils of war in direct violation of God's command. Subsequently, when Israel tried to capture the small town of Ai, the townspeople rose up and killed about 36 of Israel's soldiers. It was the nation's first defeat since crossing the Jordan River, and the hostile natives "chased the Israelites from the city gate as far as the stone quarries and struck them down on the slopes. At this the hearts of the people melted and became like water" (Joshua 7:5).

Now, Achan's sin was not Joshua's fault, but Joshua did fail to handle the tragic situation with either strength or courage. Instead, this is how he responded:

> Then Joshua tore his clothes and fell face-down to the ground before the ark of the LORD, remaining there till evening. The elders of Israel did the same, and sprinkled dust on their heads. And Joshua said, "Ah, Sovereign LORD, why did you ever bring this people across the Jordan to deliver us into the hands of the Amorites to destroy us? If only we had been content to stay on the other side of the Jordan! O Lord, what can I say, now that Israel has been routed by its enemies? The Canaanites and the other people of the country will hear about this and they will surround us and wipe out our name from the earth. What then will you do for your own great name?"
>
> —*Joshua 7:6-9*

The Lord's reply was quick and to the point. God said to Joshua, "Stand up! What are you doing down on your face? Israel has sinned; they have violated my covenant, which I commanded them to keep. . . . That is why the Israelites cannot stand against their enemies; they turn their backs and run because they have been made liable to destruction" (Joshua 7:10-12). With that, the Lord gave Joshua instructions about how to recover His blessing. To his credit, Joshua got up off his face and did what the Lord commanded. It was not easy, but he did it—and because he did so, because he rallied his strength and courage, he won both for himself and for his people the inheritance promised by God.

Is there anything *you* need to claim as your own? Have you taken charge of the spiritual climate of your home? Have you consciously set the spiritual direction in which your family is traveling? Does your family have a clear picture of where you would like to take them in their walk with God? Could they explain it to others? Are you being strong and courageous in the spiritual life of your family?

Dads, God has given us a spiritual charge to lead our families—every bit as much as He gave Joshua a spiritual charge to lead Israel. The general needed strength and courage to fulfill his responsibility, and so do we. We need to claim what is ours.

*Few things will sap a man's strength faster than comparing himself to others he admires.*

2. *Joshua needed to declare in faith what he believed God wanted to do through his life.* It was crucial for Joshua to proclaim publicly what God was doing in his heart privately. In Joshua's situation, that meant speaking out that God had told him to cross the Jordan River when it

seemed impossible and claim land that belonged to war-like pagans. The people around him needed to hear that God was working in his heart, and Joshua needed others to keep him accountable to what the Lord had told him.

We must live by the same principle. We have to declare in faith what we believe is our spiritual heritage. We don't do this as if it were some kind of magical formula that causes our spoken words to take shape in the material realm. This isn't a "name it and claim it" kind of spiritual game. We do this for the same reasons Joshua did it: to build faith in our family and friends that God is active among us, and to hold ourselves accountable to our family and friends for what we believe God wants to do through us.

Suppose you believe God wants your family to go on a short-term mission trip to Mexico to build your family's faith, even though you don't have the money. What do you do? You tell your family your conviction and move out in faith, then step back and see what God might be pleased to do through you. It's an adventure none of us can afford to miss!

3. *Joshua had to resist temptations to compare himself to his predecessor.* Few things will sap a man's strength faster than comparing himself to revered mentors. Joshua's task was daunting. Not only was he following the man who challenged pharaoh and won, not only was he taking over from the man who climbed up Mount Sinai to receive the Ten Commandments, not only was he succeeding a man who spoke to the Lord "face to face, as a man speaks with his friend" (Exodus 33:11), but he was also called upon to replace a man who was "more humble than anyone else on the face of the

earth" (Numbers 12:3). Think of it: a meek superstar! What a powerful combination!

Now, how do you follow a man like that? What do you do for an encore? Joshua knew what to do; you forget it. You carry on with the task God has given you and refuse to worry about comparisons that you can't win.

There is a continual pressure on us men to compare ourselves to other men—by the cars they drive, the income they produce, the toys they play with, the status they enjoy in a company. If we give in to those temptations, we lose the fear of God. Chasing other people's dreams robs us of our spiritual strength.

4. *Joshua had to create his own history.* The exodus was past, the conquest lay ahead. Moses had brought the people out of Egypt, but Joshua had to bring them into the Promised Land. As the general stood at the Jordan River, he had no time to think about past glories; new chapters were about to be written! The decisions he would make and the example he would set would, in large measure, determine if those chapters were to be comedy, tragedy, or high drama. His choices *mattered.* He was creating history, and what he created couldn't be undone or erased. Formidable obstacles lay ahead, and to meet their challenge Joshua needed a large supply of strength and courage.

We can be intimidated by those around us, end up aping people we shouldn't emulate, and forfeit the impact we should have. Dads, if we are going to be God's man in the family, if we are going to display the inner strength to lead our families as we should, then we must accept the challenges God gives us. That means being secure in who we are and making *our* history *count*. Our choices matter more than we know.

It was a fearful prospect for Sally and I when we became convinced God wanted us to move our family into Amsterdam's red-light district. Many friends strongly counseled us against it. And there were times when we wondered if we really had heard God's voice calling us to the neighborhood. But if God calls you to do something, He will always give you the strength to complete it. We lived in Amsterdam for 18 years and can say without any hesitation that those were among the best, most challenging and fulfilling years of our lives. All of us say so—Sally, Misha, Matthew, and I. It was a tough choice, it was uncharted territory, but God had called us to that. And He gave us the strength and courage to succeed. He will do the same for you.

5. *Joshua had to refuse to check out spiritually.* Israel's commander-in-chief rejected all available escapes from the pressures of responsibility. He looked his duties in the eye and took them on. So many leaders, even in the Bible, begin well but end badly. Not Joshua. From beginning to end he shouldered the responsibilities of leadership and so led Israel through some of her finest hours. *It is how we finish that counts!*

At the end of his life, Joshua addressed his people and challenged them with these famous words:

> Now fear the LORD and serve him with all faithfulness. Throw away the gods your forefathers worshiped beyond the River and in Egypt, and serve the LORD. But if serving the LORD seems undesirable to you, then choose for yourselves

this day whom you will serve, whether the gods
your forefathers served beyond the River, or the
gods of the Amorites, in whose land you are living. But as for me and my household, we will
serve the LORD.

*—Joshua 24:14,15*

Even as an old man about to die, Joshua chose to
assume the mantle of spiritual leadership. He knew that
the real challenge facing Israel was not battles won or
lost, but commitment to God embraced or rejected. He
was a spiritual example and mentor to the very end.

Too easily we as husbands and fathers can escape
into work or hobbies and not accept the spiritual responsibilities God has given to us. We can think we are
fulfilling our role by earning money for the family, but
that is only one part of our obligation. God has charged
us men with setting the spiritual tone in our families,
and we can't fulfill that duty by concentrating solely (or
even primarily!) on earning a living. In God's eternal
scheme of things, our role as the spiritual leader of our
family is the most important part we will ever be called
upon to play.

## STRENGTH AND DISCIPLINE

Joshua understood that it is the fear of God that
gives us the strength to resist the gods of this world.
Fearing the Lord is what made it possible for him to
serve God with sincerity and faithfulness and to gain
inner strength. He understood this at the end of his

years because he had acted upon this conviction throughout his life.

In the same way, out of the inner choice we make to fear God comes the strength and resources to lead our family. If we hope to create the atmosphere God wants for our homes, it must begin inside of us. We can't create an atmosphere through rules, nor can we set the right spiritual tone in our families by trying merely to control our children's behavior.

I have known many unhappy men who believed that "strength" meant "control." They believed that being the spiritual leader meant they were the spiritual dictator. They acted as though every decision that needed to be made was theirs to make, as though they were the order-giver, commander-in-chief, and head despot.

That, however, is not strength; it is actually a form of acute weakness. Men who believe they need to control every aspect of their family's lives are filled with fear. They are afraid to let others succeed, they are afraid their weaknesses might be exposed, they are afraid the world could get along just fine without them. At bottom, they are afraid to let God be God and are unwilling to live by faith in a sovereign Lord.

Several phrases often betray such men, demonstrating their lack of strength and glaring weakness. Phrases such as:

"Don't talk back to me!"

"Don't question my authority!"

"Do it because I said so."

The problem with such phrases is that they simply *demand* rather than affirm the child and then explain what is wrong on the basis of a principle. Being strong does not mean:

- covering up our failures

- suppressing our feelings

- demanding our own way

- having no close friendships

- making all the decisions

- controlling everyone's behavior

- leaving religion to women

It may be that this problem of control comes out most strongly in the issue of discipline. How we discipline our children demonstrates more about our own character than we may care to admit. Controlling, dictating dads don't make good disciplinarians, and they don't produce healthy, God-fearing children. It takes strength to discipline in a godly way, and controlling dads don't have it.

Godly discipline takes place in a home only when it takes place in the heart of a man. Discipline is the overflow of a vital, growing relationship between a man and his God. We cannot discipline our children if we have not disciplined our own walk with God.

Spiritual discipline is not a set of rules; it grows out of a relationship. It is not behavior modification; it is inspiring in our children an inner desire to please God.

It is not being the lord of the manor; it is leading your family out of the relationship you enjoy with the Lord of glory.

*With spiritual discipline, we don't focus on a child's behavior; we focus on the child's heart.*

Fathers commonly make two errors in disciplining their children: the Frankenstein approach and the Santa Claus approach. The Frankenstein approach sets rules and threatens, while the Santa Claus approach is based on bribes.

God is not looking for fathers who are eager to control the behavior of their children, but for fathers who long to give their kids an inner motivation to please God.

## LEADING THROUGH THE MINE FIELD

During the civil war in Zimbabwe, I saw giant vehicles, raised high off the ground and shaped like a V on the bottom, leading convoys from Harare to Bulawayo. These heavily fortified mine-finders were called "rhinos" and were ideally suited to lead the way. The drivers of other kinds of vehicles were only too happy to follow the rhinos, because that's where safety could be found.

The rhinos remind me a lot of dads and discipline. Discipline becomes effective when a father leads the way through the mine field of this world. He's not afraid to step out in front because his desire is to please God. That gives strength to his children to follow him. He doesn't stand behind with a whip, saying, "You walk out there, and if you get a leg blown off, I'll come and help you." He goes before and shows the way.

Discipline in the home should never revolve around bare rules. The idea is to create a focus on God in the home, a "God atmosphere" that reflects your own motivation and desire. We don't focus on behavior; we focus on the heart. It has to start from the inside. May I suggest an example?

Misha came home from her first day of high school at age 13 and announced she was going to a disco dance on Friday night. I thought, *I don't want my daughter to go to a disco dance!* But neither did I want to lay down the law in an impersonal way. I felt this was an opportunity to help her become strong in the Lord. Someday she would have to decide for herself about things like dances.

I did not want merely to control my daughter's behavior at a dance; I wanted to transfer to her a value, an inner motivation, a set of principles that could guide her decisions throughout the rest of her life. I did not want to communicate to her that jumping up and down rapidly to music was sin. I believed something much more significant was at stake.

Still, I couldn't find it in me as a father to say, "That's fine, sweetheart, just go ahead." I was deeply concerned for her welfare. I had a dilemma on my hands. I was caught between a theological conviction against rule-based behavior and a fatherly conviction of not letting a 13-year-old make a decision she was not yet equipped to make.

Therefore I sat down with her and said, "Misha, I can't say yes and I can't say no." I wanted to hear what her motivation was, then I wanted her to hear my own heart. But as soon as I said, "I'm not going to give you an answer," she exploded. She demanded an answer; she wanted an argument. She was like a four-year-old child who has had her toys taken away. She was cleverly, maybe subconsciously, trying to engage me in a conflict. I immediately recognized what she was doing and decided not to debate with her. I just said, "Sweetheart, I'm not going to argue, but I would like to talk about it." What I got was another heated response.

After about an hour Misha settled down and we started discussing her request. "Tell me why you want to go," I said. I listened to her reasons, even though I was pretty sure I already knew what they would be. I felt it was important to hear her and to be able to repeat back to her what she was feeling—the pressures, the adventure of doing something new and exciting. She wanted to go, but she didn't want to go. Yet if I didn't want her to go, she wanted to go all the more!

I said things like, "Wow, that sounds exciting. What kind of guys are going to be there?" And, "Sweetheart, a guy's hormones are bigger than his brains. I'm worried about what might happen. Are you worried?"

I wanted my daughter to know that I trusted her, but that as a father I was also concerned for her well-being. I believed she would find great security if I led her to make a decision based on inner strength of commitment to God. And even though the process was a bit threatening to a 13-year-old, it would help her to establish a framework from which she could grow securely into her femininity. I was convinced the interchange would give her inner strength and would set an example that she could follow later on.

I began asking her the sorts of questions that I wanted her to have in her toolbox for the rest of her life. I asked, "What will the atmosphere be like? Do you think it will be helpful to you? Who will be there? Do you want to be with them? Why do you want to be with them? Will it be fun, or will it go over a certain line and stop being fun and become destructive? What would make it destructive? What could keep it fun?"

We continued the discussion for two or three nights and finally I felt she understood my concerns. By then it was Thursday night, one day before the dance. I said to her, "Why don't you pray and ask God what you should do?" At first she replied, "I don't want to do that—I don't think God will let me go." But I insisted, "Well, you go ask Him. Just pray about it."

I realize that is a bit risky for some parents. I know some people would say, "You can't ask God something like that!" But I wanted Misha to develop an inward motivation to please God. I wanted this to be *her* decision—with my help! I also believed there would come a time in her life when she would ask God about decisions like this and God would simply reply, "Well, what do you want?" I wanted her to experience that first under my tutelage, within the confines of my care.

She came back the next day and said, "Daddy, I think God said to me I'm not ready." With great relief, I responded, "Oh—OK." Inside I thought, *Praise God!*

Her conviction lasted for a little more than a year. Twice during that time we had the same conversation with the same result. But when she was 15, after another long conversation, Misha said to me one day, "Daddy, I really think God said it's OK for me to go to the dance." I expected that to happen sometime, so I replied, "OK, Mish, but because I believe God guides us by wisdom, I would like an older friend of your choosing to go with you. I have to approve her, but you make the choice. She can be a fun-loving person, but she needs to be a solid Christian."

Misha chose an older girl from our church who was a solid Christian, a young woman who really enjoyed life. She was a lot of fun to be around—young, about 19, a pastor's daughter who dressed fashionably. The kids all liked her. So I said, "Fine, you can go together."

Misha went, she came home, and didn't say too much about the event. I was dying to hear about what happened, but she wasn't volunteering any information. This happened again at the next dance about three or four months later. I was very nervous. Finally, it came out. After the second or third dance, she said, "Dad, I don't want to go back. I don't like it." "Why not, Mish?" I probed. "Well," she said, "guys are fighting, they're putting alcohol in the drinks. It's not fun."

Her response came out of an inward motivation, not by conformity to a rule. As a young Christian, she didn't enjoy something that was destructive, violent, or unhealthy. When she saw kids doing things they shouldn't have been doing, she made her own decision not to return. It confirmed for me that I was giving her the tools she needed to thrive in an adult world. My intention all along had been to create an arena for her to develop inner strength, then lead her into it.

I have told this story many times to mixed audiences of parents and teenagers, and it always provokes some fascinating dynamics. The kids needle their parents to give them more freedom, while the parents glare at me for daring to tell such a story. But the story isn't intended to illustrate license versus legalism or freedom versus fetters. I tell the story to show that it is possible to create a home environment that doesn't depend on rules to nudge a child closer to loving Jesus. I also tell it to demonstrate that doing so isn't easy.

## But What If I've Done It Wrong?

It's easy for us dads to feel like failures. What if we are leading by "behavior control" and all we're getting is violent reactions? We've tried to control our children's behavior and they have resisted our attempts. Maybe we're even trying to control our wives. We don't like what they do and so we try to modify their behavior ... and the result is increased tension and a profound sense of failure. It's just not working.

Or suppose we have a domineering wife and we react to her nagging by trying to change her behavior. Or maybe we have no control over our kids because we are away at work 10-12 hours a day. It seems like every day we run into anger, rebellion, wrong values, and attitude problems. If that describes us, how in the world are we going to bring discipline into our home? What is going to work for us?

One thing is for sure. If we try to control our family's thoughts and behavior, we are not leading through

the fear of God. We're trying to lead through domi-
nance, and God doesn't use that method.

> *Love without discipline is
> indulgence, and discipline
> without love is tyranny.*

Sometimes the potentially negative experiences in
our home are actually opportunities for deep bonding
between a man and his children or a husband and his wife.
If we respond out of humility, out of the strength that
comes from fearing God, it can lead to a breakthrough
in the relationship. Allow me to relate one example.

My son, Matthew, was sitting in the front row at a
church meeting. A missionary was speaking, and he
droned on and on. Everyone was getting bored and
looking at their watches. Finally, Matthew couldn't take
it any longer. My 14-year-old son spoke up and publicly
rebuked the man for speaking too long! When I heard
about this later, I was horrified. I went to Matthew and
said, "Matthew, what did you say?"

"He asked if anybody had any questions. And I had
a question: 'Why are you so boring?'"

"Well, yeah, but Matthew—you said it publicly!"

"Dad, he asked if we had any questions."

Somehow I had to respond to the situation without
alienating my son. He is a very concrete thinker who
needs to hear good reasons for an argument. You can't

merely appeal to emotion. He has got to be convinced, and he must be convinced with what he knows to be true. He has to see the principle behind your point.

So I said to him, "Was the guy boring?" "Yeah, he was boring." "Do you think he spoke too long?" "Yeah, he went way over the time limit. Haven't you always said that a good speaker doesn't go longer than 45 minutes and that church should be over at a certain time?" "Yeah." "Well, he was really late, wasn't he, Dad?" I had to admit Matthew was right. The speaker was seriously late, and he truly was boring. So I said, "Well, Matthew, I think you have a good point."

But after I let my son know I had heard the truth of his words, I asked him, "How do you think you should have responded?" Together we walked through a proper response, and then I said to him, "Matthew, I want you to go to the man and apologize. If you would like, I will go with you to support you. But you need to go." He did want my support, and we did go together to apologize.

That whole, unpleasant experience bonded us closer than we had ever been. We drew close through the incident because I was willing to walk through it with him. Because I feared God in the situation, I was able to help my son. There have been plenty of times when I didn't do it right, but this was one instance where I looked to the Lord to help me.

## THE MARRIAGE OF LOVE AND STRENGTH

Love and strength go hand-in-hand in discipline. Loving acceptance and firm discipline give our children a secure foundation for growth. Love without discipline is indulgence, and discipline without love is tyranny. Both love and discipline must work together. Loving discipline both requires and demonstrates great strength.

Discipline often means confrontation. It takes strength to confront and to do it effectively. It does not take much strength to confront in the wrong way—with anger, condemnation, mockery, or manipulation. It takes real daring and fortitude to confront lovingly but firmly. In so doing, we set an example.

Loving discipline pushes the child in the right direction and challenges his or her imagination. A strong father's leadership, guidance, and discipline gives children the courage to take risks themselves, to grow, to develop in a healthy way, to choose proper behavior, and to move in the right direction.

## TAKING STANDS

A weak man does not inspire. He's insipid. Women and children feel distant from that kind of man. They feel he is uncaring, uninvolved. If he does not express strength at home, he provides no example to motivate and inspire them to follow God. A man who intends to stand for what he believes might find himself getting involved in areas of tension or conflict. He might be forced to take leadership over his children's relationships.

This kind of strength in the home does not lead to an all-controlling father who demands that the little lady and the kids serve his every whim and fancy. Nor does it mean he should exclude his wife in making decisions. There can and should be real partnership in leading the home. Leadership is not a power seesaw. Strength allows a man to lead with integrity and to lead confidently out of his inner person.

Exercising *man*power properly will encourage a woman to respect her husband's leadership. She in turn will be more effective as a wife and mother, because she won't be trying to cover for what he is not doing. Instead, she will enjoy security in her activities. She will not have to do the job of two people (and resent her husband for it).

I believe marriage is primarily a partnership in which both the man and woman have God-ordained roles to play. If a man does not play his role—if he resigns, backs out, is too busy at work, comes home tired and doesn't get involved—he will create a vacuum that his wife must fill. Inevitably, that creates tension.

## WHAT DO STRONG FATHERS PRODUCE?

Fathers who lead their homes out of inner strength produce daughters who like their femininity because dad is secure with them and relates to them as women. He draws out their femaleness. But if dad is weak and distant, they grow up unsure of themselves, insecure in who they are.

Boys growing up without a strong father also struggle with insecurity. Often they become driven and performance-oriented. They have to prove to their dad that they are OK so they can gain the approval that a weak dad fails to give.

A strong, loving man awakens his wife's femininity. She feels affirmed and accepted and loved. She does not have to compete. Strong men inspire their wives to be secure in their personalities and in their contributions to life and Christian service. When a man is secure in his identity, he frees his wife to be secure in hers. She can also confront her husband and know that he will not be threatened. She can disagree and know there will be honest exchange. She can freely express her opinions and emotions without apology or fear.

Joshua was a man who took seriously the challenge to be strong and courageous. As a result, the nation and family he led prospered.

It's too bad that Rehoboam, a subsequent leader, didn't follow Joshua's example. When Rehoboam was crowned king after the death of his father Solomon, Israel was at a crossroads and desperately needed strong, courageous leadership. Sadly, it didn't get it. Rehoboam had the choice to lead wisely or to play dictator, and he chose the latter. Out of weakness, he told the people, "My father made your yoke heavy; I will make it even heavier. My father scourged you with whips; I will scourge you with scorpions" (1 Kings 12:14).

Foolish words, destructive words. From that day on, the nation split in two. And Rehoboam's house was left in shambles.

Men, it's up to you to take up God's challenge to be strong and courageous. Joshua took the challenge. He said yes. He stepped forward.

Will you?

# ___ ACTION STEPS ___

- From Joshua we learned that it is how we *finish* that counts. How would you like to finish in life? Write this on a three-by-five card and place it where you will be reminded of this goal daily.

- Discipline of children is not merely a set of rules; it is inspiring in our children an inner desire to please God. Set aside a time alone with your wife, over a cup of coffee or tea, and ask yourselves: Does our discipline inspire our kids to please God? What changes can we make to encourage such a result?

- A strong, loving husband awakens his wife's femininity and helps her to feel affirmed, accepted, and loved. Schedule an evening out this week at a nice restaurant of your mate's choice, and let her know how deeply grateful you are for her!

- A strong, loving father helps his children to grow up secure of themselves and knowing they are loved. Take time today to verbally affirm your love for each of your children. Back up that affirmation with a hug!

# 4

# A Warm Man in a Cold World

Shortly after I became a father, I visited the home of a good friend. He was cuddling his little eight-month-old in his arms, getting ready to put her in bed. I'll never forget his words. I had never heard a father speak like this to a child. The warmth of his words blew me away. He said things like, "You're mine. I want you. Nobody can take you away from me. You belong to me. I love you!"

The scene lasted only a few moments, but it taught me an unforgettable lesson. I learned that *warmth* is an essential characteristic for a husband and a father. It is a manly, masculine trait that gives tremendous strength to his family and provides a massive support framework for everyone in his home. By his warmth, a father says to his wife and children, "I like you. In fact, I find you irresistible."

## THE WARMTH OF GOD

Communicating with warmth is a reflection of the character of God. There is a fascinating Old Testament passage that I think all fathers would do well to consider. Psalm 103 is a powerful song of praise to God, lauding Him for His goodness, justice, and holiness. The middle of the psalm describes His compassion in language that ought to pique the attention of Christian dads everywhere:

> As a father has compassion on his children,
>     so the LORD has compassion on those who fear him;
> for he knows how we are formed,
>     he remembers that we are dust.
> As for man, his days are like grass,
>     he flourishes like a flower of the field;
> the wind blows over it and it is gone,
>     and its place remembers it no more.
> But from everlasting to everlasting the LORD's love is with those who fear him,
>     and his righteousness with their children's children.

> *—Psalm 103:13-17*

A bachelor friend of mine once used this text to preach a Father's Day sermon. He reasoned that, although he had no experience as a father and would have no worthwhile advice to offer dads, he *did* know someone who could give expert counsel: the heavenly Father.

He picked this passage because it not only tells us that God has compassion on His children, it also tells us *why* He does so. The Lord has compassion on us because:

1. *He knows what we are made of.* God doesn't harbor unreasonable expectations of us because "he remembers that we are dust." Dust is our native soil, so to speak, and we often reflect our place of origin. Fathers who take this to heart can't help but become compassionate. They remember that their kids aren't perfect—that they're prone to mistakes and pratfalls—and will take special care to deal with them gently.

2. *He knows we are fragile.* In God's eyes, we are as frail as a blade of grass, as delicate as a desert flower. We may think of ourselves as oak trees, but God knows better. A dad who remembers his kids are fragile will be deliberate with his words and actions, knowing that a father's angry outbursts or harsh attitudes have the power to wilt the "flowers" in his family just as surely as a scorching sun will shrivel the flowers in his garden.

3. *He knows our lives are fleeting.* Our days are like summer grass, springing up and disappearing in one brief, fleeting season. A dad who understands that his kids won't be around forever will try to develop deep compassion. He will strive to take advantage of the very short time he has to guide, enjoy, and love his kids. They grow up so fast, then they're gone. There is no way to regain those precious, brief years of childhood. A wise father will remember this and go out of his way to show compassion both to his wife and his children.

Psalm 103 reminds us that God's compassion flows like a rushing stream to those who fear Him. When we're thirsty, when our throats are parched with the difficulties and disappointments of this world, He invites us to drink freely from His cool, refreshing, inexhaustible supply of love and compassion. In fact, He *delights* to refresh us in His love, as Psalm 147:11 reminds us: "The LORD delights in those who fear him, who put their hope in his unfailing love."

It may surprise some people to learn that this theme is highlighted throughout the Old Testament. The prophet Hosea, speaking for the Lord, wrote, "It was I who taught Ephraim to walk, taking them by the arms; but they did not realize it was I who healed them. I led them with cords of human kindness, with ties of love; I lifted the yoke from their neck and bent down to feed them" (Hosea 11:3,4). That is a wonderfully affectionate appeal, full of compassionate language describing how God delights to lead His people out of bondage and lead them with infinite warmth.

And how could I fail to mention Zephaniah? "The LORD your God is with you, he is mighty to save," the prophet consoles his nation. "He will take great delight in you, he will quiet you with his love, he will rejoice over you with singing" (Zephaniah 3:17).

The Lord loves to show compassion to His children—and a man who fears the Lord will follow His example. Unfortunately, some of us have trouble grasping what this might mean for us. It goes against the grain of our society. Our culture's stereotypes insist that warmth is for sissies—for feminine, emotional (maybe gay) men, while real men are big, burly, and macho. "Don't come sniveling around *me*," such men snort. Hugging another man is foreign to these men. Their emotions are often locked up inside, and the result is they come across hard and uncaring. They actually become hard, even though they may want to be caring.

## WHAT IS WARMTH?

With so much confusion in our culture about what real love and warmth looks like, let's try to define it:

1. *Warmth is physical affection.* A man communicates warmth through a hug, a pat on the back, a little hand squeeze, a wink, or by holding hands. There is nothing more beautiful than to see a man and a woman who have been married for 40 or 50 years holding hands as they slowly work their way down the street. Everybody loves it! Why? Because it symbolizes the deep affection they still feel for each other; their hearts are with each other, permanently woven together.

Physical warmth can be communicated with something as simple as starting the day with a wink or a hug. And the rewards of such simple physical displays go far beyond what you might expect.

In *Dealing with the Dad of Your Past,* author Maureen Rank reported the results of a survey of highly promiscuous women who were asked to identify the outstanding characteristics of their fathers. These women invariably chose words such as "coercive, hateful, unlikable, distant, threatening." Rank writes,

> Without fatherly affection, a girl comes
> to believe that her hunger for touch can
> only be satisfied in one context: that of

sexual encounters. This hunger for non-sexual touching never received from their fathers, gnaws at many women. It can get them trapped in marriages and sexual relationships that they never really wanted.[1]

A lack of fatherly physical affection can cause both boys and girls to escape into mental fantasies of sexual indulgence. Warmth expressed through a father's physical touch can prevent such a tragedy.

2. *Warmth is kindness.* A man communicates warmth to his wife and children by helping out in the home and by playing with the kids spontaneously when they clamor for his attention. A dad communicates tender love when he drops his newspaper or walks away from the news just because his kid comes running into the room and says, "Hey, Dad!"

---

*A woman never tires of hearing the words, "I love you."*

---

A man who opens the door for his wife, who writes little notes to her, or who comes home with flowers and a smile at the end of the day when he is tired, shows he is going the extra mile. These small expressions of warmth add up to much more than the sum of their parts.

Another way we men can display a real sense of tenderness and warmth is by communicating in detail what happened to us during the day. Most men probably don't like to communicate details—at least, *this* man doesn't. But my wife loves it! I once heard someone say the difference between a man and a woman is like the difference between headlines and fine print. When I come home, it's an outright effort for me to say, "It was a great day. We worked hard, but we got the project done." But Sally isn't satisfied with bare bones; she wants the whole roast. "Floyd," she will plead, "tell me what *really* happened. What went on? Please, talk to me!" She doesn't want the headlines; she wants the details. A tremendous bond is created between us when I take time to communicate with her in detail. She's deeply appreciative of this simple gesture of warmth.

3. *Warmth is tender words.* A woman never tires of hearing the words, "I love you." Children cannot be told enough that they are cherished and wanted. Watching how your wife and kids are doing, understanding what they are going through, and then speaking the right words of understanding or support or appreciation all communicate tremendous love.

If we dads anticipate the needs of our family and we are really listening when our wife and children talk, then we will communicate genuine warmth. If we express appreciation for the mundane, everyday things— the laundry, the ironing, the meals, transporting the kids—we affirm and strengthen our family relationships. Even a phone call in the middle of the day can express affection: "Hi, Babe, I was thinking of you; how are you doing? I will be home late." It doesn't cost us much, but you couldn't buy the tremendous benefits it pays.

4. *Warmth is praise.* A godly man never tires of giving encouragement. He has basked in God's affirmation and approval and out of that rich storehouse he distributes freely to his wife, his children, and his friends. Because he fears the Lord, he is unconcerned what others may think of his public or private efforts at encouragement. He praises his son's intentions to do good, even when the little guy makes big mistakes. "Nice throw, Bud; try it again!" he shouts when his boy's effort at throwing the football in a nice spiral looks much more like the Hindenburg wobbling to earth. I can remember my own dad doing this with me when I took apart a radio to see how it worked and was unable to put it back together!

Seeing a child's good intentions or inquisitiveness and praising those intentions is incalculably important. It's critical to praise a boy's maleness and a daughter's femaleness and their natural interests and gifts. This encourages them to take pride in who they are and gives them a sense of satisfaction and well-being. Praise builds esteem, confidence, and a strong bond of friendship. Spoken words can build or destroy. Our tone of voice can set in motion feelings of confidence or condemnation—feelings that last for a lifetime. You can choose your words, but not their consequences (*see* Proverbs 10:11).

The Bible says a man is the head of his home, and one translation of the term rendered "head" is "source" or "fountain." That suggests that one of the best ways to provide headship is to lavish encouragement, life, and blessing on our family members, just as a mountain stream lavishes cool water on the plants and animals it nourishes, bringing them life and vibrancy. Praise is one big way we can do this. We can crush children with angry, impatient words, or we can release hope and creativity through words of praise. By believing in our children and by expressing our conviction, it's hard for us dads to go wrong. Kids who grow up in such a home build great confidence and are willing to take risks.

Loren Cunningham, the founder of Youth With A Mission, is the most safety-conscious man I have ever met. I think that is the biggest reason we have had so few accidents in the history of the mission. Loren doesn't like staff people driving through the night because he feels it is unsafe. He is Mr. Safety Conscious.

At one of our big outreaches during the Montreal Olympics in 1976, I went to visit Loren in the trailer he and his family were using. As I approached the front door I saw his six-year-old son, David, dangling in the branches of a tree some 30 or 40 feet above the ground. It scared me to death. I quickly found Loren and said, "Loren, David's about to kill himself! Come quickly!" I expected him to bolt outside and retrieve his endangered son. I received a great surprise.

Loren calmly strolled outside and said, "Hey, David, how you doing? Wow! Oh, man, am I proud of you! You climbed all that way! Great! Well, son, when you are ready to come on down, we've got some supper for you. OK?"

Magic words! *Vroom!* David was down in a flash. Loren got David out of a dangerous position without taking away any of his confidence for daring or risk. Then he looked at me and said, "You know, I want my kids to take risks. I just want them to be *reasonable* risks." That made a lasting impression on me. David was in a

risky position, but all Loren did was praise him...
and wisely appeal to his little boy's taste buds.

David is 23 now and is finishing his schooling at
University of Southern California's film school. He already has his own film company, is producing spots for
television, and travels all over the world. He is taking huge risks all the time—financially, by submitting
scripts, and by approaching powerful producers with
his ideas. David is a very godly young man who wants to
use his skills for the Lord. He wants to be salt and light
to those around him. He leads a Bible study for producers and media people in Los Angeles, and people
just seem to flock to him. I was with him a few days ago
and it is easy to see the fruit in his life brought about by a
dad who believed in him, who praised him, and who
through his encouraging words created life in his son.

---

*Busyness never creates an
atmosphere of warmth or
acceptance.*

---

5. *Warmth is nonverbal.* A smile can do so much to
warm up a person's day. Just walking into a room and
greeting a person kindly with a warm look of appreciation can change a bad day into a good one. Loren used
to tell me, "Floyd, I can tell when you are worried and
upset. You furrow your brow and you walk around totally absorbed in what is worrying you. Try to look at

people, smile at them, and take time for them. It will make a world of difference in your ministry."

I have watched him closely through the years, and he practices what he preaches. A crowd of people always approaches him after he speaks at some event. Immediately he is surrounded with a flock of listeners and VIPs pulling at him. But if a young person asks him a question, he will turn down the world for that kid. Very rarely will he break eye contact. He bathes that young person with a warm, open look. When that young person walks away, he is floating on cloud nine because this important man believed in him and took time for him.

Such nonverbal signals communicate that you think a person is important, significant, and has great value. You dignify a person and empower him. How important it is for us as men to put the paper down, turn off the TV, and look into the eyes of our children! I once read of a study which reported that the average father has an average of three minutes of eye contact with his children each day. I repeated this information publicly several years ago at a meeting where my daughter Misha was sitting in the audience. Thereafter, all through high school, she would come home from school, throw herself in my lap, tear the newspaper away from my face, and say, "I WANT MY THREE MINUTES!"

6. *Warmth is taking time to put your family first.* Busyness never creates an atmosphere of warmth or acceptance. Warmth says, "You are important to me; you are more important than a golf game or a night out with the boys." Warm dads take care not to send signals that

they are busy or distracted—that something else is more important than their family.

All of us grow frustrated and irritable with those who shunt us aside. I get very annoyed if I am on the phone with someone who has call waiting and he interrupts our conversation to say, "Excuse me, just a second." I hate it. Normally I have to plan my phone calls, so being interrupted throws my schedule out of whack. I think, *Just get rid of call waiting! Don't do this to me!* Have you ever been put on hold only to have your party never come back to you? Or has a switchboard operator asked, "Would you mind waiting?" and then put you on hold without waiting for your response? Those kinds of things irritate me because they don't communicate personableness, importance, or respect.

How do we put family first? We schedule them in. They are more important than playing golf, than church meetings every night of the week, than our favorite TV program, than hanging out with the guys, than an extra job. Our kids are worth the extra time, even if it means fewer toys or a smaller house. They are with us only a short while, and spending time with them is an eternal investment in people created in the image of God.

7. *Warmth is merciful actions.* God is a restoring God. He takes problems and crises and redeems them. In the strictest sense, God has never faced a problem. He doesn't see problems; He sees opportunities to demonstrate His grace and mercy. No situation is ever out of His control; He is never challenged in the way we are. God loves to be redemptive. Every bad thing God turns around and uses as an opportunity to bring about great good. One of the most redemptive verses I know of is

Genesis 50:20, where Joseph declares to the brothers who so cruelly abused him, "You intended to harm me, but God intended it for good...."

God's man in the family strives to look upon the problems that inevitably crop up as an opportunity to show his wife and children the redemptive character of God. He looks for ways to teach them that they can always go to God with a problem and that He is there to help them solve that problem. In fact, God's man learns that God often allows the problems—or in some cases, purposefully causes them—for our teaching, growth, refinement, and for building into us the qualities a child of God must possess.

If a husband and father doesn't believe in redeeming crises, he will not be a merciful man. He will not see problems as an opportunity to build, redeem, restore, and teach. He will see them merely as problems, and so only sees half the picture. He doesn't go the full step, the whole way.

When my family moved into Amsterdam's red-light district, I went through a spiritual test in my heart. I couldn't help but think, *What if my daughter ends up becoming a prostitute because we live in this neighborhood?* The question seems foolish to me now, but back then it weighed heavily on my soul. *What am I doing,* I thought, *exposing my kids to this?*

From somewhere the phrase popped into my mind, "My kids could never make me stop loving them. There is nothing they could do to make me stop loving them." I knew that was true because I know there is nothing any of us can ever do to make God stop loving us.

From that day on I often repeated those words to

Misha and Matthew: "You can't do anything that would ever make me stop loving you. If you face a crisis, I'm committed to you. I may struggle with it or react, but I'm committed to you. This is not negotiable. Whatever happens, I'm going to go through it with you. You can never get rid of me! I'm committed to you."

I believed it was important for me to communicate this as a reminder of God's basic commitment to His people. He just doesn't give up—not even on prostitutes. You don't believe me? Then look at the genealogy of the Messiah Himself.

Toward the beginning of the list, which appears in Matthew 1, you will see this notation: "Salmon the father of Boaz, *whose mother was Rahab*" (verse 5, emphasis added). Flip back to Joshua chapter 2 and you will meet this lady. Two spies had been sent out from Israel's camp to survey the Promised Land and "they went and entered the house of a prostitute named Rahab" (verse 1). It was this "lady of the night" who took her place as an ancestor of Jesus the Messiah!

But that's not all! Matthew 1:3 mentions "Judah the father of Perez and Zerah, *whose mother was Tamar*" (emphasis added). Tamar wasn't a prostitute by profession, but she once impersonated a hooker to get her father-in-law (Judah) to sleep with her (*see* Genesis 38). Even Solomon's mother, Bathsheba, is mentioned in the genealogy as she who "had been Uriah's wife" (Matthew 1:6), thus commemorating the fact that both of Solomon's parents had been adulterers.

This genealogy alone should convince us that no sin—sexual sins included—is able to move people beyond God's redeeming grace. God loves us, He waits for us, and He redeems us. His merciful actions speak volumes about His compassion, and we dads can't afford to ignore His example.

## THE CALL TO CREATE WARMTH

This idea of creating warmth in the home isn't just a good idea; it's a command—and it's necessary for the healthy development of our families. Ephesians 5:22-33 contains some of the most extensive "marching orders" for Christian dads found in the whole Bible. This is that famous passage about husbands loving their wives and wives submitting to their husbands. Unfortunately, we often concentrate so heavily on the first few verses of that passage that we neglect the rest.

I think we need to consider some lesser-known words of the apostle Paul: "Husbands ought to love their wives as their own bodies. He who loves his wife loves himself. After all, no one ever hated his own body, but he feeds and cares for it, just as Christ does the church" (verses 28,29). The words "cares for" in verse 29 come from a term that means "to create warmth" or "to warm." It's the same term used in 1 Thessalonians 2:7, where Paul wrote to the believers in Thessalonica, "We were gentle among you, like a mother *caring for* her little children" (emphasis added). The great apostle knew the critical importance of showering warmth upon the people he loved. The same principle holds whether you are trying to build a church or a family.

We dads are called to build a warm fire in our homes through our love, acceptance, kindness, and encouragement. God's man in the family looks for ways to fill the emotional cup of his children and spouse. Warmth shows people we care—more effectively than almost anything else we can do. There is truth in the statement, "People need people in order to be people. People need people in order to want to live."

> *Love and acceptance are*
> *what will motivate our kids*
> *to be all they can be.*

Kids don't need to be perfect; they need to be loved. Most "underachievers" are really victims of "over-expecters" who somewhere along the way have forgotten about love and care—in other words, about warmth. Love and acceptance are what will motivate our kids to be all they can be, not unrealistic expectations. Dads who are committed to showing warmth want their kids to shoot high, but they are also there when their kids miss the target. These dads become real good at reloading!

Dads, it is our privilege and our responsibility to create the kind of security in our homes that will draw out the gifts of everyone in our family, then to cause those gifts to flourish and develop in a natural environment of encouragement, trust, and release. Warmth is central to that whole process. And dads who learn to show warmth know firsthand the deep and lasting joy that so thrilled the psalmist when he wrote, "The LORD delights in those who fear him, who put their hope in his unfailing love" (147:11).

## ═══════ *ACTION STEPS* ═══════

- Read the first two paragraphs of chapter four again. Are you, too, a warm father in a cold world? Do you show this warmth to your children daily? There are many ways to do so...with a chat over breakfast...a hug or kiss before you leave for work...praying together before the young ones go to school...five minutes of your undivided attention as soon as you get home from work. Think of some other expressions of warmth, and put one or more of these into action *this week.*

- It's healthy for your children to see you express warmth and tenderness to your wife. Can they tell how much you care for her? For example, you could give her a hand with one of her evening chores, bring home flowers, or talk with her lovingly at the dinner table. Write a list of ten simple gestures of warmth, pick one you would like to do today (in front of the kids!) and begin making them a pattern in your family life.

- When was the last time you wrote a short, simple love note to your wife? Write one...and "hide it" somewhere that she will find it during the day.

- Write short notes of affirmation for each of your children as well, and place them in a surprise location, too.

# 5

# The Cry for Involvement

Some years ago a Spanish boy named Paco ran away to Madrid, the capital of Spain. He fled to escape the emotional pain of living at home with a father who treated him cruelly. One day his repentant father went to Madrid to search for his son. He put an ad in the paper asking Paco for forgiveness for the hurt he had caused and pleaded for his son to come home. The ad asked Paco to meet his father at a certain time and a certain place on a certain day. At the scheduled place and time, Paco did show up—*along with 800 other young men named Paco.* Just think—in one city alone, 800 young men named Paco were living separated from their fathers. How many were there with other names, in other towns?

## THE CRY FOR INVOLVEMENT

High school students in Fresno, California, were

recently asked, "If you could change anything about your family, what would you change?" Thirty-nine percent said they wanted to get along with their parents; 39 percent said they wanted to be able to talk with their parents; and 35 percent said they would like to spend more time with their parents. These kids were crying out for more time with mom and dad.

And no wonder. A few years ago, Boston University asked fathers how much time they spent with their children. The fathers guessed they probably spent an average of 15–20 minutes a day with their kids, but when the school taped hidden microphones to the children, it was discovered that the average father had 2.7 contacts a day with his children for a total of *37 seconds* on the average.

Absentee dads, whether they are absent physically, emotionally, spiritually, or psychologically, cannot build friendships, cannot instruct their children in the ways of God, cannot be available when they are needed, cannot teach and coach their kids in skills, and cannot provide strength for godliness.

Sons and daughters long for their fathers to be involved in their lives and to be active and present and positive forces in the fabric of their day-to-day experiences. When have you ever heard a child say, "What I would really like is an uninvolved, distant dad"?

A friend once said to me, "I want my kids to enter into my world someday, and I have decided the way to do that is to enter into their world now to build a bridge." Entering into the world of my wife and kids and involving myself in their lives in a way that respects their freedom and encourages their growth is a huge nonnegotiable for me. I don't want to be an absentee dad!

Occasionally we read in the newspaper about parents abandoning their children on the steps of an orphanage or in a plastic bag in a shopping cart. I read last week about a baby who was left in a parked car and a rat bit the infant so many times that the child bled to death.

Abhorrent as these acts of desperation and cruelty are, it is equally destructive for children to be abandoned emotionally. Uninvolved dads scar their children psychologically and send a message loud and clear: You are not important to me.

## THE PROBLEM OF DEFAULTING DADS

Some men consciously leave all interaction with their children to their wife or to other kids. Two weeks ago I met a girl at a youth camp whose parents were sending her to a different camp every week during the summer, except for two short stretches when no camps were available. During those little time gaps she was to be shipped off to her grandparents. She was not allowed to come home once during the summer. Her parents were moving to a different town in September and it never occurred to them to tell their daughter where they would be living. Talk about one very insecure teenage girl with an absent father!

Children with emotionally absent fathers show many of the same behavior patterns as kids of divorced parents. I have a friend, "Sharon," who was abandoned by her father and mother when she was a child. While her mother moved down the street two houses away and began living with another man, her father became an alcoholic. The overpowering feeling that still haunts Sharon to this day is abandonment. A tremendous void continues to plague her.

Absent fathers create in their children an inner void, a vacuum, an emptiness. Psychologists call it a "love deficit." Children don't feel believed in and they don't feel ready for life. A strong relationship between a dad and his kids helps teach children discernment: how to make judgments about relationships, how to deal with conflict. An involved dad gives his kids confidence in relating to other people. And if dad isn't around, a child—especially a young girl—can grow up vainly searching for deeply satisfying relationships that promise to meet that need.

Extremes in behavior are the result when young women don't enjoy a caring relationship with their fathers. You begin hearing statements like "all men are rotten," or you see young girls jumping in and out of relationships at a frenzied pace. Or you see the idealization of a father: "Daddy is perfect." Girls transfer this fantasy of the father they never had to all men and seek a dream partner, only to be dissatisfied with every suitor who shows a serious interest. Multiple, painful marriages are often the result.

We urgently need dads who choose to be involved in the lives of their wife and children. There is a tremendous sense of abandonment that comes from the absentee men in this nation. The challenge for all of us as dads is to consciously and purposefully move into the world of our family members in order to give them a firm foundation for a long, godly, fulfilling, and successful life.

## INVOLVEMENT AND INCARNATION

Another way to say we are involved is to say we are *with* someone, and nobody was ever *with* someone more than Jesus Christ was with those to whom He ministered. One of His biblical titles is "Emmanuel," which means "God with us." God was not content merely to send us instructions for living or tips on godliness while He Himself remained aloof in heaven, a billion or so light-years removed from this planet. No, He purposefully determined to take on flesh, to become one of us, and to live and move and breathe elbow-to-elbow with the rest of us earthbound men and women.

> *The best way to mold your wife and children into the image of Christ is to be involved with them—go with them into that great adventure.*

Jesus is God with us. He set the preeminent example for involvement in people's lives when He came to earth. He left what was His, gave up His rights, and made others His priority. And when He wanted to instill in His followers the godly character and wisdom they would need to help Him build His church, He did so by spending prodigious amounts of time with them. Mark 3:13,14 says, "Jesus went up into the hills and called to him those he wanted, and they came to him. He appointed twelve—designating them apostles—*that they might be with him* and that he might send them out to preach" (emphasis added).

Jesus called His disciples to be *with* Him—while He ate, while He taught, while He walked, while He rested. He was involved with His men at the nitty-gritty level of everyday human interaction. Why? Because He knew that was the best way to mold and shape His disciples for the great task that lay ahead of them.

The apostle Paul followed this same pattern. When he was in Ephesus, he "*took the disciples with him* and had discussions daily in the lecture hall of Tyrannus. This went on for two years, so that all the Jews and Greeks who lived in the province of Asia heard the word of the Lord" (Acts 19:9,10, emphasis added). Notice the results! Because Paul took the time to be with the disciples, multitudes living in a vast territory heard for the first time the good news about abundant life in Jesus Christ.

Men, there is no substitute for us being *with* our wife and children and for involving ourselves in the ordinary events of their day-to-day lives. If our goal is for them to be conformed to the image of Christ, we must go with them into that great adventure. We cannot merely point the way from the reclined position of our easy chair.

A friend of mine told me of a conversation he overheard between two businessmen flying to a sales conference. "You know," said one of the men, "it occurred to me the other day that I really should consider making some adjustments to my schedule. I have been gone from home three-and-a-half years out of the last five, and I'm not even sure I know how old my kids are. Maybe I need to get to know them better."

*Maybe?* Dads, there is no substitute for ongoing, personal involvement in the lives of our children. No matter how successful we may be and no matter how esteemed we might be in our company or community, our wife and kids need us. And when we are there for them, we need to be *available*.

By the way, *involvement is not merely living in the same house,* as if proximity were the same thing as interaction. If it were, a big rock could be your best friend— it hangs around all day. But involvement requires action, response, relationship, and time together. It demands a conscious, determined effort to get into the nooks and crannies of a person's life—yet without violating his or her individuality.

God wants this same kind of involvement in the lives of His own children. Moses' passionate challenge to the nation of Israel rings with the language of involvement. Listen to his call:

> And now, O Israel, what does the LORD your God ask of you but to fear the LORD your God, to walk in all his ways, to love him, to serve the LORD your God with all your heart and with all your soul, and to observe the LORD's commands and decrees that I am giving you today for your own good?
>
> —*Deuteronomy 10:12,13, emphasis added*

Notice that healthy involvement begins with the fear of the Lord. A man who fears God has his eyes securely fixed on his Master, who wrote the book on involvement. And because such a man walks with the Lord, he can sense when his involvement has grown either too intrusive or too distant. A man who fears God and walks with Him finds that his love for God naturally grows through the years. And because he loves Him, it is no great burden to serve Him. It is no hardship to serve those in whom we delight! And how are we to serve Him? Moses tells us: with all our heart and with all our soul. Now, *that* is involvement! That is the kind of involvement that reaches down into the remotest crevices of our being—the kind of involvement that springs from a deep, heartfelt, genuine love.

This kind of all-encompassing involvement, of course, is to be reserved for God alone. But a man who fears God in this way and who allows that fear to shape his love and service will likely find that his relationships with his family take on a godly echo of his rich and loving communion with God. He will love to be involved with them because he is already deeply and passionately involved with God.

Still, it is crucial that we *consciously* permit our walk with God to shape our relationships with family members. It doesn't necessarily happen automatically. King David was a great man who dearly loved the Lord, a man who was called "the apple of [God's] eye" (Psalm 17:8) and "a man after [God's] own heart" (1 Samuel 13:14)—yet he failed to enter the world of at least one of his sons and thus became partially responsible for the tragedy which ensued.

The book of 1 Kings opens with David "old and well advanced in years" and getting ready to pass on the crown to one of his sons. Solomon was his choice, but his eldest son, Adonijah, decided he would beat his younger brother to the punch and declare himself king. Eventually his ungodly desire to occupy the throne would cost him his life.

Adonijah's story is a sad one, but it never had to happen. Had David chosen to fully enter the life of his son, perhaps the misery could have been avoided. But the text explains Adonijah's reckless actions with this note: "His father [David] had never interfered with him by asking, 'Why do you behave as you do?'" (1 Kings 1:6). In relation to his eldest son, David was an absentee father. He failed to significantly enter Adonijah's world . . . and the young man paid for his dad's neglect with his life.

## WHAT IS INVOLVEMENT?

How do we become involved? How do we measure involvement? How do we know if we are as involved in our children's lives as we ought to be? Three simple concepts help describe "involvement" for me.

1. *Presence.* The key thought here is "available." Dad is present, he is around, he is there. He is not a stranger in his own house and when he is home, he is not lost in the newspaper or stranded in network news.

It is no accident that so many preachers' and missionaries' kids are openly hostile to the faith of their parents. Children need their mom and dad to be *with* them. Our first evangelistic duty is to our own family; what have we accomplished if we gain the whole world but lose our own flesh and blood?

What does it mean to be present? It often means sacrifice. You come home from work late after leaving the house early, you are dead tired, and the last thing you feel like doing is listening to the gibberish of an excited four-year-old. What you really want to do is banish the kids, put your feet up, and retreat emotionally into the beckoning arms of your favorite chair. But a dad who decides to be *present* with his kids realizes his children need both his physical *and* his emotional presence. So he makes a sacrifice—a big one, a sacrifice that takes a lot of effort. He rallies his strength, takes a deep breath, and with a quick prayer for divine resuscitation, takes time to *be with* his kids.

There are no magic formulas that I know of, no six-ways-to-be-present-while-getting-all-the-rest-that-you-need. Being a good dad involves a commitment to making the necessary sacrifice, even when we don't feel like it. No, it's not easy. But it is worth it, and it is part of the job description for being a godly dad...and only real men need apply.

2. *Communication.* It's possible to be present physically but absent emotionally. A dad who commits himself to being involved with the members of his family will naturally want to communicate his love for them. He will look for ways to express his love, to show his support, and to apply correction when necessary. He makes sure that the love in his heart is relayed to the ears of those whom he loves. That takes communication, which is tremendously difficult for some of us dads.

A number of helpful books have been published in the past few years on how to improve communication between husbands and wives and children. One of the best, in my opinion, is Gary Smalley and John Trent's *The Language of Love*. Their book gives extremely helpful guidance on how to develop patterns of clear, effective, and encouraging communication. It's also a lot of fun! Scores of examples are cited which help to "nail" the principles under discussion. I highly recommend it.

*We'll never do it perfectly, but we'll always do it together.*

3. *Approachable.* A dad demonstrates his commitment to his family by being present to help his children whatever the problem. We could call that "being approachable." If our wife and children know they can come to us with a problem and receive help—if they know we are open and encouraging and that we are committed to them come what may—our families will grow like weeds. Stu Weber, pastor of Good Shepherd Community Church in Boring, Oregon, and author of *Tender Warrior: God's Intention for a Man*, tells his three sons, "We'll never do it perfectly, but we'll always do it together."

I had an opportunity to test this out when Misha was in high school. She was to participate in a school talent program in which the students would sing to the sound tracks of various famous musicians—a kind of pre-karaoke experience. I said to her, "I would like to attend, but I don't want to embarrass you or anything— it's possible I would be the only dad who showed up." Her first reaction was to ask me to stay home; she was afraid my presence *would* embarrass her. But as she continued to think about it, eventually she decided it would be "cool" to have me there. She has always had an independent streak and takes great delight in going against the grain, so when she started imagining my participation might make her something unique and special, she invited me to come. It turned out that quite a few parents attended.

The show featured dozens of 12- to 14-year-olds doing their best to imitate their current musical heroes. An increasingly negative sexual tone developed as the evening progressed. The last act, sponsored by the school, spotlighted a 15-year-old girl doing a Madonna imitation. It was incredibly crude. I leaned over and said to my daughter, "Misha, I'm embarrassed. I don't want to stay, but I don't want to embarrass you. I don't feel comfortable watching this." "Dad," she replied, "I don't like it either. Let's get out of here." So we left.

The next day, Misha really caught it from her friends at school. She was prepared for their criticism, however, because we had talked extensively about what they might say. That day Misha marched down to the office and complained about the school hiring such an inappropriate act. She told them she objected to the school using her money to assault her with values that were not universally held and which should not have been given such a public platform. Her comments deeply embarrassed the school officials—and I was thoroughly glad. I considered the whole unpleasant epi-sode a tremendous step forward for Misha. But it took place only because I chose to get involved in her life. I was present during an opportunity for us to discuss the issue when my daughter was at an impressionable age.

## THE RESULTS OF INVOLVEMENT

Dads who choose to involve themselves in the lives of their family members are rewarded with deeply satis-fying relationships. An involved dad provides a warm place of refuge where a son or daughter learns to love and to be loved without the complexities of sexual over-tones. They learn to trust.

Involved dads provide an emotional oasis in a des-ert of relational trauma, especially for teenagers. The teen years are so *hard*—and there dad is, understanding, accepting, affirming, listening. Tremendous security is created when a son or daughter is adored, accepted, loved, and wanted for no other reason than that he or she exists.

Dads who choose to be involved provide a shelter for a son or daughter confronted with serious conflict or hurt. Children learn to relate to adults, handle conflict, develop social skills, gain confidence for life, and emu-late values from dads who make a conscious choice to get involved in their lives.

## HOW DO I GET INVOLVED?

Many of us dads have a hard time knowing *how* to get involved in the lives of our children. Their worlds are so different from ours! So often it seems crystal clear that our kids, especially when they are teenagers, don't want us within a million miles of them, let alone in the nitty-gritty of their lives.

But I have learned (often the hard way!) that conflicts between parents and children don't necessarily mean our sons or daughters are rejecting our love or help. One of the problems is that we are intimidated by our kids and overwhelmed by our lack of knowledge, understanding, or skill on how we might be able to help. So how do we get involved when we feel intimidated or unwanted?

Being involved means taking an active interest in the things our kids are interested in and supporting them in those things. It doesn't mean taking over for them. The last thing a kid needs is a parent trying to live life vicariously through the child. A lot of Little League parents have yet to learn this principle! Becoming involved in our children's lives means identifying the emotional barriers that keep us at arm's length and figuring out ways to overcome them.

When Matthew was an early teen, he talked quite a bit to Sally, but the conversation usually dried up when I came home. I soon recognized he wasn't as open with me as with my wife. He was a challenge to me. How could I get inside of his life? How could I identify with his world? I realized I didn't have a clue how I might do that and I felt deeply threatened and intimidated by it.

I believe a lot of fathers share my predicament. They are intimidated by teenage sons or daughters. They don't know how to get past the emotional barriers or through the world of their child's peers and friends.

It's an intimidating task, given the insecure and insensitive nature of most kids. They can desperately want friendship, yet send out signals as if they don't.

So what do we do? We must gently push past the resistance, but not too hard. We have to be available in a different way for a teenager than for a toddler or younger adolescent. We have to find a common ground of interest. When there is a problem, it's up to us to find an acceptable way of offering our support. Or when our child expresses anger or frustration, we must lead the way in letting those emotions come out even while trying to get to the root of the problem without reacting emotionally to the unacceptable behavior.

But *how* do we do that? How can we deal with the inabilities many of us feel about getting involved in the vastly different and fast-changing worlds of our children?

I believe the most important beginning place is honesty. I'm sorry if you were expecting something a little more exotic! This is the only starting point I know of. We dads must humble ourselves and confess our inabilities to our wife, our kids, and our friends. We must tell them that we would like to be involved in their lives, but we need help. Vulnerability is a crucial first step to genuine involvement. Try telling your kids how you feel, and how much you would like to be a loving dad to them. Ask *them* for ways you can do a better job of being there for them.

Some of us could benefit by getting professional counsel about how to improve our ability to communicate and interact with the loved ones growing up under our roof. With that in mind, I have included an appendix at the back of this book suggesting a few guidelines for selecting an appropriate counselor. Counseling might sound like a threatening step, but I have seen it turn around a number of very troubled homes and immeasurably strengthen some other families who just wanted to grow closer together.

I would like to suggest one other way of becoming involved in the lives of our children, and that is through encouragement. Friendly, genuine compliments will go a long way toward opening closed doors into the hearts of our kids. Develop an appreciation for the music they listen to, the styles of clothes they like, their friends, movies, and so on. Then talk about these things with them. Compliment your daughter's hairstyle and your son's new shirt. Talk about a movie you watched and express appreciation for their insights.

Honesty and encouragement will go a long way toward reducing tensions and will convince your kids you truly love them.

## WANTED: INVOLVED MEN!

There is a certain kind of barrenness that comes with busyness—a certain kind of superficiality that results from running from one activity to another, from one appointment to another. A friend of mine says America is a nation 3,000 miles wide and a half-inch deep. Superficiality is rampant. We tend not to listen and we are not there when people need us. It is almost as if our kids have to make an appointment to talk with us rather than us being available so things can transpire naturally and spontaneously between us and them.

The old saying is true: "People don't care how much you know until they know how much you care." Our kids will believe we are the greatest hero on the planet if they sense that we believe in them, that we have time for them, and that we are involved with them. By our presence and our support, our encouragement and our compliments, we say to them, "You are special; you are important to me. In fact, there is no place I would rather be than with you!"

I really like Stu Weber's maxim: "We'll never do it perfectly, but we'll always do it together." A dad who lives by that simple rule is almost certain to rear children who can move into life with confidence, grace, and strength. Such fortunate sons and daughters are blessed with a bright future and a dazzling hope, and that is the kind of legacy that you can't buy at any price except one: the price of involvement.

## *ACTION STEPS*

- Even when we live under the same roof as our children, it's still possible for us to be absentee dads. Are you truly involved in their world? Do you know their friends, their interests, their favorite activities? As dads, we need to build bridges. Set aside at least one hour sometime this week (more won't hurt!) to enter your children's world with their friends or talking about and working on your children's favorite interests. Let that time become your way of saying, "You are important to me."

- Are you simply too busy to be available to your children? Write a list of what prevents you from spending time with them. Are the items on the list truly more important than your kids? What one or two actions can you take now to become more available?

- Find something in each child that you appreciate and take time to compliment or praise him or her for it... today!

- Your children's achievements are important to them, and should be to you, too. Have they won award certificates or ribbons? Get picture frames, and put the awards on display in your home. Or, start a family photo album in which you document every member's accomplishments. Get an album this week, and let it become a family project. You can add to the fun by creating homemade certificates or ribbons with the help of an artistic person or a computer.

# 6

# Seven Keys for Releasing Your Kids

One evening after I spoke in Vancouver, B.C., a mother approached me to say that her 18-year-old daughter had heard me the night before and was very interested in serving with Youth With A Mission. The mother opposed any such plan. She wept as she told me how much she needed her daughter at home and that she was having a hard time cutting the umbilical cord. She implored me to counsel her daughter against leaving home. I replied that I couldn't do that, but instead I encouraged this mother to release her daughter. I felt that was the issue.

A year later I returned to Vancouver and by that time had completely forgotten about the incident. The same lady approached me after the meeting, introduced herself, and reminded me of our conversation the year before.

"Would you please speak with my daughter and see if you can talk her into going with YWAM?" she pleaded.

"What's wrong?" I asked.

"I browbeat my daughter and manipulated her and kept her home, and now she doesn't want to do anything for God," she replied. "I am so sorry! I feel as if I made the most tragic mistake of my life."

"Well," I said, "you bring your daughter back here if she is willing to come. I'll be happy to speak with her. But I'm afraid I can't undo what has been done. I'm sorry." The daughter never did return.

This mother's dilemma illustrates one of the hardest and yet most important duties we parents face: the act of *releasing* our family members into the world. We men have a tremendous opportunity to believe in our wife and children and to create in the home an atmosphere of trust and security that encourages their gifts. We play a key role in launching and sending our children into the world and encouraging our wife to fully develop and use her gifts, both within and outside the home. A man's attitude and support is vital for sending his loved ones into the world.

I once heard this role likened to a garden. A man has a key to his family garden and he opens its gate to let out the fragrance inside. He brings out what is there by his attitude.

To be God's man means we not only let go of our kids, but we also actively encourage them to serve God. This is not a passive letting go, but an active training and preparation. This is a nonnegotiable to be a man of God. It is part of what it means to put God first in our lives as men. We present our children and our mate to God and ask Him to use them for His glory. If we don't do this, we are not really open to God's will for our lives. That is why releasing our family is so crucial for being God's man in the family.

## TOUGH QUESTIONS IN SWITZERLAND

Many years ago Sally and I spent several choice months at L'Abri Fellowship in Switzerland with Dr. Francis Schaeffer. Dr. Schaeffer customarily asked three questions of parents when they brought their children to be dedicated to the Lord. I have never forgotten them:

1. If God should take your child or allow him to die through an accident or a sickness, do you promise not to be bitter against God or blame Him?

2. Do you commit yourself to be the spiritual discipler of your children, to teach them the ways of God actively and consciously, and lead them to know Jesus Christ as their Lord and Savior?

3. And will you do everything you can to encourage your children to pursue the call of God upon their lives, laying aside any expectations or personal ambitions you have, and that if they decide to become missionaries in Christian work, you'll stand behind them in that pursuit?

Dr. Schaeffer got at the heart of what I want to discuss in this chapter. One of our fundamental tasks

as husbands and fathers is to believe in our family so
deeply that we purposefully release them into the service of God.

I believe this is one of the most difficult tasks we
fathers must perform. Releasing our "little ones" (who
are no longer so little!) is tough for many of us. We are
afraid they will get hurt. We are afraid they will make
wrong choices. We are afraid we will never see them
again. But a man who fears God—and who has done his
best to impart the fear of the Lord to his children—will
reject those earthly fears and instead entrust his kids
into the arms of their Creator—*no matter what happens!*

I think that is one of the most extraordinary aspects
of one of the Lord's most remarkable parables. Most of
us are familiar with the unforgettable tale of the prodi-
gal son recounted in Luke 15:11-32. Jesus told that story
to remind His hearers of God's unlimited love for His
creation—even for children who had rejected their heritage and gone their own rebellious way. The par-
able is one of the strongest statements about God's
grace to be found anywhere in Scripture. Yet it is also a
powerful commentary on God's commitment to releasing His own children.

The father in Jesus' story had reared both his sons
in an atmosphere of love, acceptance, and the fear of the
Lord. But when his second son reached young adulthood, he demanded to be given his inheritance so that
he might leave his father's estate and spend his money
however he chose. The father knew his son's plan was
unwise and could guess at its disastrous outcome, but
complied with his boy's rash wishes and released him
into God's care.

The son descends into a shameful pit of destructive choices, but the story ends happily when he finally realizes his folly and returns home. *But notice that there would be no story at all if the father had refused to release his son!* That father knew his son was set on a destructive course, yet he also knew the time had come to release him. And he knew one other thing as well: His boy ultimately belonged to God, not him, and it was God's responsibility to work in the young man's heart, not his. So he released him. It was that very act which ultimately led to his son's redemption.

The Old Testament also has something to say about the act of releasing. At one point in his illustrious career, Moses found himself enrolling in Releasing 101. You see, releasing is not merely entrusting our loved ones into God's care, but also encouraging them to grow in the gifts that God has given them and letting them go wherever that may lead them. Exodus chapter 18 describes how Moses was wearing himself out trying to settle disputes among his contentious countrymen. Fortunately, his father-in-law Jethro stepped in to give him a wise piece of advice: "Select capable men from all the people—men who fear God, trustworthy men who hate dishonest gain—and appoint them as officials over thousands, hundreds, fifties and tens" (verse 21).

Prior to this conversation, Moses had been unwilling to allow others to act as judges for the Jewish people. He had tried to do everything himself, and it was killing him. The solution to his problem? *Releasing* capable men—men who had been tutored in the fear of the Lord by Moses himself—to do the work. Moses had to learn to trust that God could work in the lives of others just as surely as He worked in his own. Moses took Jethro's advice, and the result was not only more rest for Israel's exhausted leader, but also scores of men who now were able to use their God-given talents to fulfill their God-ordained roles. When Moses saw the need and wisdom of letting go, he let go . . . with, I'm sure, one of the biggest sighs in Old Testament history.

> *It's easier to release our kids*
> *into the world when we*
> *believe God will watch them*
> *and He has their best*
> *interest at heart.*

Perhaps the biggest problem many of us face in releasing our own children is the issue of trust. It is hard as a father to let your children go into a world you can't control, especially if that takes them a long way from home. Yet that is exactly what God calls us to do. Releasing is really a matter of trust: Do we trust God to look after our children? Do we really believe He has their best interest at heart, infinitely beyond our own deep concern?

Sally and I had to deal with the issue of releasing when we decided to move into the red-light district of Amsterdam. We were severely criticized when we announced our intentions. People simply could not understand why we would take our children into such a dark environment. Even though we were sure it was God's will for our family, such strong criticism caused us to doubt our wisdom more than once. Yet in God's good providence, at precisely that time I began reading about the life of William Booth, the founder of the Salvation Army. Back in 1865 he took his children into the east end of London, a tough and terrible neighborhood, and reared them there. He, too, was inundated by criticism, but he responded by saying he wanted to create an inheritance for his children greater than what men normally create—he wanted to give them a lasting spiritual heritage.

Booth's words became a tremendous motivation and hope for me. I might not build a great physical estate for my children by moving into the red-light district, but I was convinced I would give them a lasting heritage of spiritual values, of love, and of mission. I would try my best to bestow upon them a commitment to base their choices about where to live not on circumstances alone, but to involve themselves in people's lives based on their need. I wanted my children to learn to serve people first ahead of themselves. I longed to bequeath to them a legacy of service to the urban poor and needy.

More than anything else, I wanted to create an arena for my children where they could step in and receive such a heritage, even if they didn't become missionaries. Their vocational choice was not my first concern. My deepest desire was that their lives would be imbued with biblical values that would motivate their direction in life. I deeply believed that we could accomplish all this by living and ministering in the heart of Amsterdam, and through our lifestyle impart to our children a love for the lost.

None of this would have transpired had Sally and I failed to make a conscious choice to release our children into God's care. Our Amsterdam experience wasn't the ultimate releasing of our children—the day is coming soon when they will leave home and follow God's call on their lives—but it was a big step in preparation for that final release. And while it was difficult, it ultimately proved to be fabulously rewarding.

## SEVEN KEYS FOR RELEASING YOUR KIDS

How do we prepare our kids for life? What steps can we take to equip them to move out into life as confident, godly, productive men and women? I have identified seven important keys for releasing our kids into a life of great challenge.

1. *We believe in them.* We believe in our children by affirming them when they take risks. We believe in our children by embracing their dreams and by showing interest in their adventures, whether they are creating a spaceship in the backyard, camping out overnight in the forest, or developing a new invention. Imagination is a wonderful gift! We are given the great privilege of encouraging our kids to think about all the things they can do, to believe in them, and to affirm them.

It is important for us to be present when our children take their risks and fail, when their adventure explodes into a thousand flaming pieces. They need us to debrief them, to talk about their feelings and their experience, to discuss what they can learn from it, and to help them move forward. Permanent emotional scars can result if somehow we are not there to offer our support and understanding.

As a junior-high school quarterback, a close friend of mine was coveted by no less than three rival high schools for his leadership skills on the football field. His first year in high school went well, as he made the varsity team along with just two or three other players his age. But things went sour the next year when, instead of a lot of playing time, he was offered a seat on the bench. His disappointment increased further when his girlfriend started dating another young man. Hurt and confused, my friend walked into his coach's office and said, "I may as well quit; I'm not needed." The only consolation he received was a curt, "OK." My friend was shattered.

He trudged home, told his parents, and to his deep dismay they said nothing. Their silence crushed him. He is just now processing his profound hurt and calls this incident a black hole in his life. What he needed that awful day was a coach who believed in him—a coach who would say, "No, son, we are counting on you. You are going to be great, but you have got to compete for playing time now. You have got to step up to the challenge." He needed a dad who would process his disappointment with him and who would discuss his dreams and his expectations and their implications. My friend's lifetime dream up to that point was to become a pro football player. His traumatic experience forced him to face the probability that he might not play as a pro. But nobody was there to walk it through with him, and that void robs him of confidence to this day.

2. *We encourage the use and development of their gifts and talents.* When my son Matthew first started showing

an interest in computers at age six, I started taking him to computer stores. He would walk up to a computer, sit down, put his hands on a keyboard, and start having fun. I, however, was totally intimidated. I would whisper, "Matthew, be careful!" Just then a salesman would walk over and remark, "That's all right, he can do that. He won't hurt anything." The salesman knew what this behavior would lead to!

The truth was, I was threatened by Matthew's ability to function in an environment totally foreign to me. Yet I determined to help him explore this new area of interest, even though I would have preferred to be just about anywhere else on the planet.

3. *We give them skills.* Children need to learn basic living skills, such as how to open up a savings account and how to save money. We used a little routine with our kids: ten percent tithe, ten percent savings, and ten percent giving to the poor. It was hard work for one of our children, while the other one thrived. We helped them get checking accounts and asked them to work out budgets. We explained expenses and income and how important it was that the two items be fairly related to one another!

We also worked to give our children people skills. We instructed them to greet people warmly, to look them in the eye, to shake their hand and smile at them. Again, this was easier for one of our children than for the other. We believe it is an important social skill to be able to greet people graciously and to sit down and talk to them without causing great discomfort.

When Matthew and Misha were ten and twelve, they were given the opportunity to work in a Christian bookstore. They ran the cash register, helped stock the shelves, greeted people, and learned their way around the store. This built tremendous confidence in both of them. They developed important social skills, learned how to count money, and received a little training about business.

Sally and I also tried to give our kids skills at thinking critically by discussing the day's news around the dinner table. "What happened? Why did it happen? What do you think God thinks about it? What would God want you to do?" We tried to get the children to think and to develop skills of discernment. We would often discuss people and their behavior: "What do they do? How do they relate to others? Do you like the way they do this? Why do you like it? How should we react if we don't like it?" We looked for as many avenues as we could think of to encourage our children's growth in discernment and wisdom.

4. *We discuss training and educational opportunities with them.* We should take care not to miss the creative moments during which to encourage our children's gifts. Matthew likes to write, and when he was 13 a friend who was hosting a writer's seminar invited him to attend the three-week clinic, even though it was geared for adults. Matthew loved the seminar and wrote a little science-fiction piece as part of the course. I don't know if my son will choose writing as a career, but we felt it was important to encourage him to take advantage of the opportunity.

Every child marches to the beat of a different drummer. Some are creative, some are concrete; some are fast, some are slow; some are introverts, some are extroverts; some talk out what they are learning, some internalize the learning process. Unfortunately, our educational systems usually cater to only one kind of child. I think that is one of the great tragedies of American education. Dr. Francis Schaeffer used to say, "I will never let school stand in the way of my children's education." He took his kids out of school once a month for special outings as a family to do something unique for their learning. They would visit a museum, read a book together, or attend a special event. Life was always an adventure, a learning expedition.

Some of us must restrain ourselves from imposing our vocational expectations on our kids. Imposing our choices on our children can create an unnecessary crisis for them. They don't need that kind of pressure. We should not grow frustrated if a teenager doesn't yet know what he or she wants to do. That's OK, there is time for that. A real education helps them explore the various opportunities open to them.

The whole idea of moving from high school to a university to a job is inappropriate for some kids. That routine doesn't fit everyone. There are a lot of excellent personality tests available that help children become aware of their personalities and personal vocational possibilities. We obtained such a test for Misha through her school in Holland. When the results came back, she went down the list of options and said, "No, that one's not me. But I would like to do this." So we talked about it. We didn't so much believe that we needed to make definite plans, but we wanted to assist her in thinking through what was out there and how she could go about getting to where she wanted to be.

5. *We feed our kids biographies that inspire their dreams.*
Kids need heroes, not mere celebrities. Rock stars are
celebrities, but that doesn't mean they are heroes. A
movie star is famous, but not necessarily a hero. Even
some preachers are celebrities without being heroes.
We need to look for heroes: people who do great things
to help others and who, through their character and
their example, show us a more excellent way. Martin
Luther King, Jr. is a hero for many of us. Winston Chur-
chill is a hero. Don Richardson is one of my heroes.

Kids need heroes besides jocks and movie stars and
musicians. It's part of our job to help them find some.
And one of the best ways to do that is to open the world
of books. Through books, our kids can enter the lives of
great men and women of God. I have given my children
missionary biographies to read since they were toddlers.
These books have helped make my children aware of
the vast opportunities that exist to make a difference in
the world.

6. *We discern what God is doing in the lives of our wife
and children, and cooperate with Him.* Admittedly, that is
a bit subjective, but I think it's vital. Sometimes we im-
pose a spiritual agenda on our family members that
God doesn't share. I believe God sets the pace of our
spiritual development by selecting an area of personal
growth for His special focus. A wise father tries to be
sensitive to the Holy Spirit's efforts at helping his children grow in a certain area. He must ask himself, "What
is God trying to do in the lives of my children? What
area of character weakness is God trying to change?
What spiritual lessons is God trying to teach them?"

There was a time as a little girl when telling the truth became really hard for my daughter. Misha habitually exaggerated more than I found acceptable. Soon the issue started popping up all over: People began confronting her; relationships began breaking down. Sally and I sensed this was more than a natural stage and decided it was time to help Misha appreciate truth and how much it meant to God. So we tried to cooperate with God by focusing our own attention on the matter.

This does not mean we should rescue our children from every difficult situation they face. Sometimes they need to go through pain to gain. I don't believe we should always step in and solve conflicts between siblings. Sometimes we should say, "Kids, we would like you to go to the bedroom and solve this yourselves. Come back when you can tell us how you've worked it out." In that way we put the responsibility on *them* to cooperate with God.

7. *We affirm the unique personality of our children and wife.* God creates people to be different from one another. They approach life differently, they make decisions differently, they process information differently, they react to pressure differently. They have differing emotional makeups. If we appreciate the differences of our children and our wife and respond to them accordingly, our ships will sail much more smoothly on this great Sea of Family. And they will grow up feeling positively about themselves and about serving God.

For example, God has created Sally to be a concrete thinker. She is extremely thorough, detailed, and process-oriented. On the other hand, I am highly task-oriented and concerned about the bottom line. The process isn't nearly as important to me as is the goal. I allowed our differences to create a lot of conflict in the early years of our marriage—and sometimes I still do. When I finally began to see that God had created her to be different from me, I started to understand her need for thoroughly processing decisions. I began to see and appreciate how she approached the future and her spiritual gifts of teaching, exhortation, and hospitality. At last I began to enter into the process with her and affirm her and the decisions she was making about how she was going to serve God and other people.

Sally is a principled person and will ask a hundred questions about every decision we make. I used to think that was unbelief and saw her pragmatism as a negative quality. Finally I began to see what a wonderful gift it was and how much I needed it. My change of perspective encouraged Sally in her self-image. She began to see that she had a real strength and that she had an important contribution to make. My new attitude affirmed her and released her to serve God and others in a way appropriate to her makeup.

## A TRAP TO AVOID

As men we have a unique opportunity to prepare our children to venture boldly into life unencumbered with man-made rules or fear or the need to be rescued. If we follow this principle in life, the fruit will be a family open to serving God and family members who trust God and are eager to do whatever He asks of them. But there is at least one big trap along the way that we need to recognize and avoid.

Our love is necessary for the healthy growth of our kids, but there is a kind of overbearing love that some kids get hooked on. They become emotionally dependent on us and can't leave us when it is time to go. It can also work the other way around: A father can become so dependent upon his children that he doesn't want them to move away. By his attitudes and actions he communicates that kids who *really* love their parents will not live more than a day's drive away from home. I have seen that a lot, and it's tragic.

Some men like being Mr. Wonderful. They like those little adoring eyes and they can't break their addiction. I know an evangelist who adopted this as one of his supreme values. He passed it along to his kids and built into their lives a control mechanism to enforce it. One of his children went into the pastorate but soon got divorced; later he committed adultery in a second relationship. The evangelist's daughter married, had kids, then got a divorce. Today she is a sad lady. Another son married a non-Christian and now deeply regrets it.

In an unwelcome and unexpected sort of way, that pastor got exactly what he wanted. All of his kids live close by mom and dad—and all three are uniformly miserable. I have talked to all three of his kids, and all three have ignored a call of God upon their lives in order to stay close to dad. They are Christians, but they are desperately dependent and unhappy Christians.

Dads, it's all too possible to bind our kids to us by creating false needs and then meeting them so that no one else can match us. We can love too much; we can meet too many needs. We can create "The Perfect Dad Syndrome." It may seem ideal, but it will only end in tragedy. As men and fathers, we are to *represent* God, but not to *become* God. That's idolatry.

---

*The greatest love we can lavish upon our children is to train them in the fear of God, equip them for life, and then release them.*

---

There is a profoundly sad and deeply moving chapter in C.S. Lewis's little fable *The Great Divorce* that describes an encounter in heaven between a redeemed spirit and a deceased mother. The unhappy woman belligerently demands to see her only son, who had died some years before:

> Give me my boy. Do you hear? I don't care about all your rules and regulations. I don't believe in a God who keeps mother and son apart. I believe in a God of Love. No one has a right to come between me and my son. Not even God. Tell Him that to His face. I want my boy, and I mean to have him. He is mine, do you understand? Mine, mine, mine, for ever and ever.[1]

Lewis, through another character, then writes,

> What she calls her love for her son has turned into a poor, prickly, astringent sort of thing.... There's something in natural affection which will lead it on to eternal love more easily than natural appetite could be led on. But there's also something in it which makes it easier to stop at the natural level and mistake it for the heavenly. Brass is mistaken for gold more easily than clay is. And if it finally refuses conversion its corruption will be worse than the corruption of what ye call the lower passions. It is a stronger angel, and therefore, when it falls, a fiercer devil.[2]

Our children do not belong to us, but to God. The greatest love we can lavish upon them is to train them in the fear of God, equip them for life, and then release them into the world at just the right time.

## THE POWER OF BELIEF

The key to preparing our children for the day of their ultimate release is our passionate belief in them. That is why I listed "believing in your children" as the first of the seven ways to prepare our kids for release. Never underestimate the power of your belief!

A church in Redding, California, invited 57 kids to a ski camp at Lake Shasta, featuring the theme of radical discipleship. The camp was designed to interest kids in the church, and most of the campers didn't know the Lord.

I was there to present two one-hour talks each day. The camp was full of young rebels who had zero interest in the church; they just came to water ski. One of these tough youngsters was a 14-year-old girl. On the third day of camp I looked straight at her and said, "Jeanette, you are a real leader. I really think you're something. You're going to change the world."

My statement shocked her. She did not know what to think. So I continued, "I am impressed. When you speak, wow, people follow you. But Jeanette, there's only one problem."

"What is it?" she asked.

"You're leading them the wrong way. And it's going to kill the adventure. You're not going to have fun."

Already she was hooked. I had her.

"You're going to get so bored with what you're doing because you're going the wrong way," I continued. "You're going to lose the adventure; it's going to lose its excitement and fun."

"What do you mean?" she demanded.

"Well, you're trying to have fun doing all the wrong stuff, and all the wrong stuff is boring. All the wrong stuff just doesn't work. It turns people against each other and quickly loses its fun. It's empty; it doesn't work for long. Listen, Jeanette, I've traveled in 125 countries. I've been all over the world for God. I'm helping to change the world for God. I have seen people come to know God and get their lives sorted out. I have seen whole nations affected through our work. Why don't you come and lead with me? I want to challenge you to be a leader for God."

She didn't know what hit her. The idea blew her out of the water and she became my shadow for the rest of the week. What was it that turned her around? It was a matter of getting inside of her heart, then getting out in front of her and giving her a challenge. I hoped to create in her a hunger for God, an expectation, to implant in her the idea that she could be somebody who could do great things for God. My belief gave her the inner strength to say no to hurtful things.

I believe that is what God says to us through the cross: "You are important. You can do what I call you to do. You are somebody I died for. You're not merely a worm. In My hands, you can do great things for Me."

Our belief can go a long way toward readying our children for that great day when we release them into the wild, blue yonder . . . to do great things for God. It's a day that ought to fill us with both great anticipation and tremendous hope. The Bible calls our children arrows in our quiver (*see* Psalm 127:4,5), and it's a vastly comforting thought to consider that any arrow released in His service speeds toward its target buoyed up by the gentle wind of His Holy Spirit. If you like bull's-eyes, this is how you get them.

## _____ ACTION STEPS _____

- All of us as dads have regretted something we said or did. Perhaps you have found yourself wishing you had shown more love . . . laughed more often . . . listened more carefully . . . prayed more faithfully . . . encouraged more frequently. No matter what our children's age, however, there is always time. Consider a shortcoming you would like to change, and share that one-on-one with each of your children. Tell them how you plan to improve on that shortcoming in the days ahead... they will appreciate your honesty more than you may ever know.

- Are you preparing your children for life by helping them to find heroes that are worth imitating? A good way to do that is through books. Take your children to a bookstore this week and help them find stories about great people who have made a difference. If you can, you may want to get stories about great men and women of God.

- Preparing children for the future includes giving them practical skills. Find something around the house that needs fixing, and make it a family project.

# 7

# He Who Has Ears to Hear

Many years ago Sally asked me to sit down with her to talk about some difficulties she was experiencing. I listened for a few brief moments, quickly solved her problem (in my mind, at least), interrupted her, and informed her of my conclusions. She looked me coldly in the eyes and told me she already knew the solution; she just needed someone to listen to her! She reminded me that I was not behind a pulpit nor did I need to solve her problems for her.

"Floyd," she said, "I'm sharing with you because I need someone to listen to me, to comfort me. If I can't talk to you, who *can* I talk to?" She said that out of frustration and out of deep hurt, and her words hit me like a hammer between the eyes. *She's right*, I thought. *If she doesn't talk to me, who will she talk to? Is my failure to listen driving a wedge between us? And what about my children? If they can't talk to me, who will they talk to? And what about the people I pastor and lead? If they can't talk to me, who will they talk to? Where will they go? Am I the kind of man, father, husband, and friend that people know they can talk to without getting preached at?*

At that moment, the value of listening suddenly became vitally important to me. Sally's rebuke stunned me out of complacency. I'm just sorry she had to slap me with a two-by-four to jar me awake.

## WHAT IS GOOD LISTENING?

Good listening progresses from accepting a person—unconditionally—to understanding what he or she is saying, and then supporting him or her in the search for solutions to the problem. From acceptance, to understanding, to hearing, to solution. There are absolutely no shortcuts to this process. *None.*

Listening is a lifeline into a person's soul. It is a window into a person's inner being, into his or her real self. Good communication creates a word window to allow us to see inside others and to know what is happening within them. As a person opens up the window, we must listen or we will fail to understand what is going on.

Without listening, *we will grow apart* from those whom we love. *Conflicts will go unresolved* because we won't hear their correction or their encouragement. *Friendships will die.* We will *lose the comfort* that people want to give us. We will *miss great wisdom, guidance, and intellectual stimulation* simply because we are not fully hearing what people say.

## A LEADER IS A LISTENER

We dads have to be listeners if we are going to be leaders in the home. It's not a bad idea to periodically ask ourselves, "How many minutes a day do I actually spend listening to the important people in my life?" In fact, let me suggest that right now you take out a pen and a piece of paper, look back over the last week, and count up how many minutes you spent actually listening to each child and to your wife. Think of those times when the TV and radio were off, the paper was down, and no music could be heard in the background. It was just you and that child or you and your wife. They had 100 percent of your attention and you heard them. You not only heard the words, but the meaning as well. How many minutes like that can you identify?

I don't mean to motivate anyone by guilt, but our families are too important to be shunted aside. They need and deserve more than the frazzled leftovers of our time. Our wife and kids are the most valuable things we have outside of the Lord, and too many of us act too frequently as if that weren't the gospel truth.

Listening is a divine trait. Did you know that? God often describes Himself as a listener. In fact, it takes our conscious, willful sin to *prevent* Him from listening (*see* Isaiah 59:2). He even listens when we don't realize that's what He is up to.

Malachi 3:14,15 recounts the harsh charges that some of the people of Israel were bringing against God. Malachi then writes:

> Then those who feared the LORD talked with each other, *and the LORD listened and*

*heard.* A scroll of remembrance was written in his presence concerning those who feared the LORD and honored his name. "They will be mine," says the LORD Almighty, "in the day when I make up my treasured possession. I will spare them, just as in compassion a man spares his son who serves him. And you will again see the distinction between the righteous and the wicked, between those who serve God and those who do not.

—*Malachi 3:16-18,*
*emphasis added*

How miserable we would be if God did *not* listen! We count on His attentive ears every bit as much as did the psalmists, whose pleas for mercy and help crowd Israel's ancient hymnbook like trout in a breeding pond. God is our great example. He is the One of whom the psalmist said, "He fulfills the desires of those who fear him; he *hears their cry* and saves them" (Psalm 145:19, emphasis added).

A man who fears the Lord not only expects His Savior to hear and act on his cries for help, but he also follows his Savior's example. He, too, is attentive to the cries of his loved ones. He listens to them because God listens to him. A Christlike man strives to become like the Master, who was a master listener.

## ONE MODEL OF COMMUNICATION

Listening is an integral, irreplaceable part of effective communication. A number of years ago linguist

S.I. Hayakawa developed a simple but effective model of communication. Hayakawa pictured good communication as a process between the speaker, the listener, and the grid through which messages are transmitted. The graphic below illustrates his model:

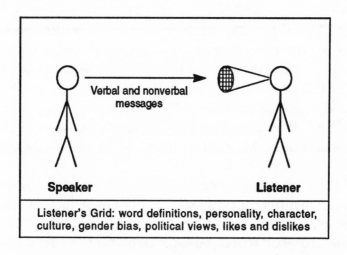

Speaker      Listener

Listener's Grid: word definitions, personality, character, culture, gender bias, political views, likes and dislikes

In good communication, a message is sent from the speaker to the listener with the listener receiving substantially the same content and meaning as was intended by the speaker. How important it is for the listener to give feedback to the speaker in order to ensure that he is hearing what is actually being said! It's amazing what our "grid" can filter out.

Men, it is critically important for us to create an atmosphere in our homes in which our children and our wife truly believe that we want both to hear and understand them. Listening is hard work! Our grid tends to filter out all kinds of critical information, and some of the "static" is gender-based. It's very true that men and women often don't speak the same language.

## A MAN AND HIS WIFE

According to authors Gary Smalley and John Trent in *The Language of Love*, the average man speaks roughly 12,500 words a day while a woman speaks 25,000 or more. For most families, that means the man comes home having used up all but about 50 words at work. His wife, however, is just getting warmed up! She has used only half her quota. Men figure they get paid to talk all day, so they want to be quiet when they come home. They don't want to talk all night. Naturally, this can lead to conflict.

There are other significant, gender-based communication differences as well. For most men, facts are the major part of conversation. Smalley calls this "fact talk": baseball scores, box scores, batting averages, who got traded, stock prices, housing prices. Facts make for black-and-white thinking and mostly clinical interaction. A man's relationships are built primarily around facts, and fact talk keeps emotions bottled up between a man and his wife.

Women prefer what Smalley calls "heart talk." They tend to express feelings of love, frustration, concern, and joy; they are not content to stick to the bare facts. This is especially true as it applies to resolving conflicts.

If we earnestly desire to develop close relationships with each of the members of our family, we must go to the heart. Failure to do this inevitably leads to superficiality. However, "heart talk" doesn't happen all at once. There are several steps leading up to it. Perhaps it would be helpful at this point to describe six basic levels of communication that characterize our relationships, from casual ones to the most intimate.

## SIX LEVELS OF COMMUNICATION

1. *Silence.* Grunts, groans, and mumbles populate this lowest level of communication. I'm thinking of the sounds that only men seem capable of making, noises designed to dodge conversations they don't want to join. Picture a husband getting up in the morning and grunting his way to the breakfast table, "Uh-huhing" his way to the door while he pecks his wife on the cheek. He's task-oriented and he just wants to get out there and do his job. He is tired when he comes home, so he picks up on the same level. Clearly, this does not make for deep relationships!

2. *Clichés.* At level two we use little words and phrases that have no meaning, such as, "Well, whatever you would like to do, dear." "If that's how you feel." "Let's talk about it sometime." "Is that right?" "Well, I'll be darned." "That's nice, dear." Clichés have moved from unintelligible sounds to actual words, but it's not really much of a climb. You will never build a deep relationship with this kind of communication, but you will likely provoke a volcano in your spouse.

3. *Facts.* Facts move beyond empty words to convey actual substance, but it is substance without soul. A computer can do as much: "It's that far, it costs that

much, these are the results." Facts make possible important and necessary communication, but they don't yet explore who a person is in-depth. Facts are still outside of the person.

> *A wise man will stimulate his family to think from a biblical point of view.*

4. *Ideas.* This is the first level that starts to get inside a person. Ideas tell us what people think, what they believe. Ideas go beyond mere facts. The fact could be, "The pastor's sermons are too long," while the idea is, "I'm not sure how many people are able to stay awake while the pastor drones on and on. And I'm positive I don't agree with what he taught today about the rapture."

Ideas are important in a family. They stimulate us and cause us to wrestle with unfamiliar concepts. A wise man will open the door wide to ideas of many shapes and sizes, stimulating his family to think, especially from a biblical point of view.

5. *Emotions.* Emotions are one of the big keys for opening up who we truly are. They are like the gauges on the dashboard of a car, telling us what is happening inside the engine. Those gauges aren't the engine, but they indicate the condition of the engine.

Why should we take emotions seriously? Why should we give names to the feelings bubbling up inside us?

Because they are an indicator of what is happening in a relationship. They help to tell us what is transpiring between ourselves and others. Emotions can't tell us if our response is correct or godly; they simply indicate the kind of reaction we are having. And that's valuable information.

I grew up in a home where we didn't try to describe our emotions. We reacted and simply went on. I didn't learn how to deal with feelings or even how to identify feelings until I got to Afghanistan and began working with emotionally scarred kids. They would say things like, "I hate my father" or, "I can't stand Nixon" or, "I don't trust America." All of a sudden I found myself reacting emotionally to their words. And as I heard them describe pain, rejection, fear, hurt, abandonment, and mistrust, I was confronted with my failure to identify with my own emotions. I had never taken them seriously, and now I had to.

It was a tremendous step for me. No longer would I pattern myself solely after my parents or be restricted to their mode of response. Now I began to think through how I ought to respond. Soon Sally and I started to grow in our relationship. She began telling me how she felt about my treatment of her. I also realized that I couldn't help the kids in Afghanistan unless I took their emotions seriously. Eventually I concluded that we can't grow spiritually unless we identify how we feel.

Don't get me wrong. How we feel will not promote growth; rather, it allows growth. Emotions don't give us the answer; they simply give us a description of what is happening inside. Labeling our emotions allows us to go to God and say, "I was hurt and I'm angry and I can't stand that person." Only then can we go on to say, "God, will You forgive me and help me to forgive?" Only then do we know we need to forgive and that we need God's help to respond in the right way.

6. *Secrets.* At this intimate level we share our innermost secrets, dreams, experiences, fears, guilt, and needs. I can say to my wife, "You hurt me," but if I go down deeper and say to her, "I need you, and I wish that somebody would know that I have felt this way for a long time," then I'm starting to get down to my secrets, to who I really am, to what I treasure in my heart.

Different men communicate at different levels. I know men who never make it beyond level 4, the realm of ideas. I've heard of others who never venture beyond level 3, the telling of facts. What a terrible waste, what a sad rejection of our full humanity, and what a loss for the family! Only those who dare to launch out into the deep waters of levels 5 and 6 (our emotions and our secrets) will be rewarded with the rich and satisfying pleasures found in intimate communion with another person made in God's image. Those are waters worth exploring! And what wonders and treasures they harbor! Sure, there is risk involved; but no one ever enjoyed a deep-sea adventure by paddling around on an inflatable duck in his neighbor's backyard wading pool!

## HOW TO COMMUNICATE WITH YOUR CHILD

Effective communication with your children is a different kind of challenge than communication with your wife. Allow me to suggest several practical guidelines on how to do it well.

1. *Establish eye contact with your children.* Let them know that they have your undivided attention. Don't switch back and forth between them and your watch. Stop what you are doing and look them in the eye.

2. *Use a physical posture that tells your children you are there with them.* It can mean getting on your knees, sitting down, or putting them on your lap. It definitely means turning away from what you were doing. Many kids see a father who hides behind a newspaper, slouched down in a chair or couch, retreating from the day's busyness. He doesn't have time for them. His very posture says, "Don't even bother."

3. *Listen.* Listen not only to the words, but also to the meaning behind the words. Listen to what is *not* being said. Listen to the tone of voice and watch the facial expressions.

4. *Ask sincere questions.* Think of questions that help the child communicate his or her: a) feelings; b) experiences; c) expectations; d) ideas.

5. *Reflect back to the children what you hear them saying.* Don't do this in a clinical way, but do make sure you are hearing them properly and that they know you hear them. The goal is to make them feel understood.

## UNDERSTANDING MISBEHAVIOR

Good communication, of course, does not guarantee our children will always behave like little angels. But misbehavior is often a clue about the quality of our communication. Our children sometimes misbehave because they think we are not listening to them. They don't feel understood or accepted. According to child psychologist Dr. Wayne Light, all misbehavior can be traced back to one of four reasons:

1. *Desire for attention.* Parents feel annoyed when this happens. A child demands interaction from a father or mother and interrupts what they are doing to get it.

2. *Control or power.* Sometimes children try to get their parents to enter into a power struggle. Children see this as an opportunity to challenge authority, and if they successfully engage their parents in a struggle for power, they actually seize authority.

Most parents don't realize that if you enter into the power struggle, you have already lost. At that point, the child is actually leading you. Imagine that you tell your son to turn off the TV. He says no, throws a temper tantrum, and you react to the tantrum. At that point, he is dominating the direction of the relationship. Kids learn this kind of misbehavior rather quickly.

3. *Revenge.* A parent does something that the child resents and the child feels hurt, so he or she does something to hurt the parent. The parent then becomes hurt by the child's vengeful actions and the child feels satisfaction at getting even, although his behavior doesn't solve anything.

4. *Insecurity or inadequacy.* A child misbehaves because he feels insecure or inadequate in some situation.

His misbehavior creates feelings of hopelessness in the parents so they react, which only reinforces the child's sense of inadequacy.

You may have noticed in all four of these scenarios that the worst thing we dads can do is to react thoughtlessly to misbehavior. Reaction is the opposite of listening. It's an emotional, mindless response rather than a careful, thoughtful one in which we attempt to understand what is creating the behavior. If we listen and discern rather than react, we force the child to take responsibility for the misbehavior.

One of my strong convictions is that we must always go beyond behavior to the heart so we can discover the root of the behavior. That's what God does with us. He tries to capture our hearts, not mere behavior. He tries to win allegiance, not control actions. He knows He will get the right actions if He wins our hearts!

I think one of the great mistakes we men make is to react to behavior. Kids know how to push our buttons. We come home tired, BAM! and we react. Then we're finished.

## SEVEN DEADLY STYLES

All of us tend to establish certain patterns of communication with our wife and children. Much of the time these patterns are healthy and productive. But sometimes they are not. The following are seven typical communication styles that actually hinder good communication.

1. *The commander-in-chief.* The commander gives orders, commands, and directs. He is insulted if people question his authority. This is a positional, authoritarian approach. If people don't respond immediately, threats and bribes are used; coercion is the norm.

---

*To be good leaders in the home, we must become good listeners.*

---

2. *The moralist.* The moralist relates to his children on the basis of moral authority. The word "shouldn't" is often a part of his conversation. The moralist is deeply threatened by irregular behavior and judges people's actions by whether they conform to his perception of right and wrong.

3. *The know-it-all.* This person doesn't listen; he anticipates conversations and tells people what they should do. Typical phrases include, "I know it, you don't." "Why are you bothering me with questions? I've already told you the answer." This person is always lecturing, advising, exhorting, and giving answers, even when they are not called for.

4. *The judge.* The judge is interested in setting himself above the common riffraff because he knows the right way. He is fond of pronouncing sentences.

5. *The critic.* The critic must always be right and is always picking at other people. He relies upon ridicule

---

and sarcasm to correct. "What a stupid thing to say!" "Nobody would do anything that dumb!"

6. *The psychologist.* This person always tries to analyze people. He asks questions in a clinical manner but has no personal concern in the crisis. He is hiding behind a mask to keep himself from revealing his own heart.

7. *The consoler.* The consoler gives simple reassurance to all problems. "It will be OK, honey. Just go out and play." He fails to take a person's concerns seriously.

None of these flawed communication styles have anything to do with real listening. They hinder true interaction and cause loved ones to grow apart from one another. All of us slip into one or more of these roles every now and then; the key is to make sure they don't characterize us most of the time.

## RIGHTS VERSUS RESPONSIBILITIES

If we dads want to be good leaders in the home, we must become good listeners. Perhaps one reason why some of us struggle with this is that we misunderstand Paul's emphasis in his instruction to husbands and wives in Ephesians 5. I'm convinced that the Lord speaks to us in the New Testament about our responsibilities, not our rights. I think men often get into trouble because they eavesdrop on what the Lord says to their wife and claim it against her, or she does the same thing to him. That always creates a demanding spirit.

But the Lord doesn't say to me, "Floyd, tell your wife to submit to you." He says to me, "Son, lay down your life for your wife." True listening means I must hear what she has to say to me—that's one important way to "lay down my life." How can I serve Sally if I never listen to what she says?

One time Sally and I were having a conflict and we finally concluded that the Holy Spirit had to be the One to bring conviction to our hearts. I couldn't convict her and she couldn't convict me. Conviction is God's job.

In this situation, I was angry with Sally and I felt as if it were her turn to apologize first. I was tired of always being the one who took the first step to admit fault.

That day I was talking to the Lord about this, trying to convince Him about the rightness of my cause, when I suddenly felt as if He asked me a question: "Floyd, do you want to be a great leader?"

"Yes!" I said enthusiastically.

"Then lead in humility," came His simple but firm response.

I immediately knew what He meant. I sheepishly sought out Sally, so I could apologize to her. I realized I had to relate to my wife first of all as a sister in the Lord, and only then as a wife. If I were to lay aside the Christian part of our relationship, all I would have left is the human shell—and that would remove all the ethical and scriptural guidelines I needed to guide me.

Men, if we want to be great leaders and be God's man in the family, we need to lead in humility. A big part of humility is the wisdom to know we don't know everything! If we want to know that which we so desperately need to know, we need to listen. True understanding comes in no other way. I'm sure it was no accident that Jesus often said, "He who has an ear, let him hear" (Revelation 2:7,11,17,29; 3:6,13,22).

# ACTION STEPS

- Instead of watching that favorite show this week, turn the TV off during that hour and give your wife and children 100 percent of your attention. Try to make more of that time *listening* rather than talking.

- A daughter once asked her dad, "How should I wear my hair today—braided or ponytail?" Her dad replied with obvious disinterest, "Do whatever you want," not realizing he had a wonderful opportunity to truly *listen* to his daughter, who really wanted his input. Commit yourself to listening carefully for similar "seemingly insignificant" opportunities for interaction— from both your wife and children. With time, you'll notice that such listening can make a significant difference in family relations!

- Review the illustration on page 145. If your wife and children could describe what kind of listener you are, what would they say? What kind of listener do you want to be?

- Do you find yourself interrupting your wife or children every now and then? Make a personal challenge to yourself to *not* interrupt...and see how long you can keep this commitment! This will show them you really care about what they have to say.

# 8

# The Fun Doesn't Start Till the Fat Lady Sings

What would birthdays and Father's Day be without the crazy greeting cards that accompany them? I love to collect the cards sent to me for these special days. They keep me humble!

For example: A few years back Matthew gave me a card that featured a sour old woman with sunglasses telling me, "It's Father's Day!" Inside she expressed the delightful sentiment, "Hope your kids don't think you're too much of a dork." It was signed, "Matthew (dork junior)."

Another year Misha gave me a card that said, "Dad! We've been through so much together—good times, bad times, fear, frustration, tears, joy, anguish, relief, and despair..." I opened the card and read, "...and that was just when you were teaching me to drive! Happy Father's Day!"

Her card deserves some explanation. One summer I was teaching Misha how to drive and the lesson for the day was backing up. We were on a side street and I was having great fun watching her practice. I thought it would be good to get Matthew in the backseat with a video camera aimed at the rear window. I talked Mish into it, but Matthew had not been in the car for five minutes when my daughter stopped and exclaimed, "Out! Finished! No more!" We had to eject the camera-man before we could continue!

Sally enjoys these cards as much as the kids. One year she gave me a card that said, "Happy Father's Day, dear! When people ask me how it feels to be married to a kind, generous person, I always say the same thing." Inside, the punch line: "Ask my husband!"

*Fun is an attitude that seeks to enjoy life and celebrate our kids.*

As you can see, my family likes to have fun. In fact, we insist on it. It's one of our nonnegotiables that, at first, might not seem so important. But I believe fun is an integral part of every growing family's agenda. Life is too short to take it so seriously! I wholeheartedly agree with the prayer of Teresa of Avila, a Spanish saint of the sixteenth century: "From silly devotions and sour-faced saints, spare us, O Lord."

## LET THE GOOD TIMES ROLL!

Fun is an attitude that seeks to enjoy life and celebrate our kids. It comes from the inside out. Some men tend to relinquish the role of "fun-meister" to their wives. But by resigning that role, we forfeit a lot of fun. It's not that we abdicate a responsibility, but we *do* back away from a part of life that God has given us to enjoy.

Discovering how to have fun is part of the learning process designed by God. He created us with a funny bone, with the ability to laugh, to have fun, to play. Besides enjoyment, fun serves a crucial purpose. It releases pressure and provides us with some wonderful bonding experiences. Some of my fondest memories are the wonderful times I've sat around with friends, all of us laughing until our sides hurt.

Life is too short to be all business and no play. An article in *Focus on the Family* magazine detailed how an average person who lives to be 70 spends his life:

- 23 years in bed, sleeping (32.9% of his lifetime)

- 16 years working (22.8%)

- 8 years in front of a television (11.4%)

- 6 years sitting at a dining room table, eating (8.6%)

- 6 years traveling (8.6%)

- 4.5 years in leisure activities (6.5%)

- 4 years sick (5.7%)

- 2 years dressing (2.8%)

- 0.5 years in church (.7%)[1]

When you break down a lifetime into its constituent bits, the good times you enjoy with friends and family become a lot more precious, don't they? Fun is not wasteful; it's productive. Fun can become a learning opportunity to teach crucial life principles. Humor provides some of the best pathways to instruction. It helps people stay in touch with themselves. It's just good mental health to be able to laugh at yourself—it helps to keep you sane.

Our best writers and speakers know this principle well. They understand it is one reason for their effectiveness. I think of G.K. Chesterton's one-liner about difficult neighbors: "The Bible tells us to love our neighbors, and also to love our enemies; probably because they are generally the same people." Or I think of the proverb you may have seen gracing the mug or T-shirt of your favorite minister: "A pastor must have the mind of a scholar, the heart of a child...and the hide of a rhinoceros."

Fun is learning. It's not an escape from development or reality, but a means God has given us to enjoy His world and to grow at the same time. Fun is the work of childhood that we're never to grow out of.

When you watch someone having fun, you get to see a whole different side of his personality. Just recently

recently I took a trip with some young interns whom I had been mentoring in a leadership program. By water-skiing with them, I saw a whole dimension of their personalities that had been hidden from me in more formal settings. It made me appreciate them much more. The father or husband who does not have fun with his wife and children is missing a delightful dimension intended by God for the growth of his family.

Fun is childlikeness. We're never to grow out of the ability to laugh and to enjoy life. People who take themselves too seriously or who are too sober soon get... well, boring.

## FUN IS FOR EVERYONE

When Sally and I were at L'Abri Fellowship studying apologetics, philosophy, Eastern religions, and Christian theology, a group of us were invited one evening to the home of opera singer Jane Stewart Smith. She looked the part—it was easy to picture her as a spear-wielding Rhine maiden in Wagner's *Der Ring Des Nibelungen*— and this was very intimidating for me. She lived in a Swiss chalet and, as a senior member of the fellowship, often hosted meals for newcomers to L'Abri.

The setting was rather formal, and as we were standing around getting to know each other, it was obvious everybody was a little nervous. Suddenly our hostess pointed at me and said boldly, "You! Would you take that book off the shelf and read it? It's an important book. I would like you to read it to us." I was startled, but I complied. As I turned around, she continued, "That green one, right there." So off the shelf I pulled *Wind in the Willows* by Kenneth Grahame.

I had never read about Toad of Toad Hall, but soon I was telling his story to a no-longer-so-nervous group of Christians and non-Christian seekers. I thought, *What a wonderful story! And what a great lady!* Oh, how she laughed! I saw a wonderful side of her personality that I never would have been privileged to appreciate had she not done the unexpected.

L'Abri taught me a lot about fun. One night a week, Udo Middleman read children's stories to us. He sat in a rocking chair and anybody who wanted to join could come. Udo has three Ph.D. degrees—in law, economics, and philosophy—and he is an exceptionally bright man with a razor-sharp mind and a lovely spirit. He is also one of the most relaxed Germans I have ever met.

So there we were, all these long-haired, serious, studious foreigners, piled in front of Udo's rocking chair. At first some listeners kept toward the back of the room, but over a period of weeks they edged forward. Soon they were just like the rest of us who were acting like little kids, sitting in a circle around Udo. He would read stories to us from the Narnia chronicles, from *Wind in the Willows,* from *Lord of the Rings.* Adults never had so much fun! And it was such a powerful witness. Everyone was immensely drawn by the personal touch, the creativity, the warmth, and family bonding this special night created.

Later, when Sally and I lived in Afghanistan and ministered to hundreds of hurting, broken kids, we quickly noticed how few of them smiled. It's hard to be hurt, bitter, and mad at God yet still smile.

In Kabul we determined that when our own kids were born, we would rear them to be creative, to have fun, to enjoy life, and to celebrate God's creation. We decided we would read the Bible to them at breakfast, pray over the day with them, and bless them. At night, we would tell stories or read good, non-Christian literature. We couldn't wait until they were old enough! We started when Misha was five or six months old, reading the Scriptures and praying and blessing her. We kept everything short. We didn't want to make it heavy because we wanted our kids to enjoy it. We wanted that time to be a blessing to them—to set a good tone for the day and for their life at school and play. I would try to make sure I was home by 5:00 or 5:30 each evening to tell stories that I had been thinking up all day!

As soon as the kids were old enough, I started telling a series of stories based on a character I made up named Wally the Whale. Wally was kind of a klutz, pretty slow, but nice. He wasn't quite sure what he believed in life. Soon there was Sammy the Shark, a real mean character, and Billy Bass, the evangelist. Billy was always trying to get Wally saved and to protect him from Sammy. We created story after story and built up lines of stories based around those three characters.

When we moved into Amsterdam's red-light district we lived across the street from an ancient church built in 1327 called the *oude kerk* ("old church" in Dutch). It was a massive, towering structure just across the canal from us. So I started making up stories about Peter the Church Mouse, who lived in that church. Peter often wandered out into the red-light district and got into all kinds of trouble. I tried to weave in spiritual values, but it wasn't preachy. We had a great time.

## WHAT, NO TV?

I once heard someone say, "The only good things on TV are the flower vase and the clock." And in the days before cable became so popular, an acquaintance of mine used to say, "You can always tell where the devil lives. It's where his tail [the TV antenna] sticks up through the roof."

Did you know that by the time an average child enters kindergarten, he has seen some 5,000 hours of TV? Those hours are gone forever; dad can never spend them with his child.

Have you ever noticed how many families seem to be undermined by television? We decided that until our kids were eight or nine years old, we wouldn't have a TV set in the house. For the first four or five years, we didn't own a TV. Television was not a part of our life. We had seen too many brain-dead kids and too many moms who were hooked on "As the Stomach Turns."

When we finally did buy a TV, it was a very special thing to watch a program—maybe one night a week, at most. That went on for many years. I believe this released the time for us to be creative and to grow in our relationships with one another.

What did we do if we didn't watch television? We went for walks as a family, we took boat rides, we went on bicycle tours, we toured in the car.

I love to explore new places. We would plan an hour devoted to nothing else but exploring. We would stop at a farm and get out to look at the animals. We met a lot of strangers that way! We would take side roads, visit museums, attend concerts, climb towers, pick fruit and berries, fish, and plan our vacations together. We studied foreign countries—nothing in-depth, but enough to learn about an interesting custom or a peculiar animal.

We did anything that stimulated the kids and allowed us to have fun together. I bought joke books and clipped out cartoons because I believed that laughing together was a great thing for my family (and I love it myself). We told jokes that we heard at school or at work or from friends.

Sally and I started telling stories about our grandparents. We described everything we knew about our heritage—the adventures they had, the hard times they suffered. My grandmother came from Norway and as a child grew up hearing and living fantastic stories about whales and bears. So I called my mom, retrieved all the stories that she could remember, and started telling them to my own kids. In that way we built a sense of heritage and family history while having tons of fun together. I told my kids about my mother's father, an entrepreneur who started a town in North Dakota, founded a bank, and became a cattle rancher.

Sally told tales about her English grandfather, a dairy farmer who became wealthy but lost it all in a hurricane in Galveston, Texas. He built up his fortune again, only to lose it all once more in the great hurricane of 1906. The only two mementos Sally has left from her grandfather are a little four-by-six-inch advertisement for his dairy that she had framed and a dining room table that a German lady gave her grandfather in exchange for some milk and a cow after the first hurricane hit.

Matthew and Misha especially loved hearing about our courtship and romance. How did Sally and I meet each other? What did we do? What about some of our early adventures with YWAM?

Don't think that you must have a resume with a dozen foreign countries listed to make your own story interesting to your kids. Everyone has stories to tell and their own adventures to describe. Kids love to hear about their roots. Your personal history may not sound terribly exciting to you, but your kids will consider it a gold mine. And it's a lot of fun to tell. A good way to start is to pull out old pictures or yearbooks from high school or college and look through them with the kids. We used to do that. We would make albums from vacations and give them to each of our children so they would have some special memory builders.

> *For spiritual fun, we kept a prayer log of the things we prayed for as a family and carefully noted God's answers.*

Sally is great at building memories. She is always celebrating special occasions with parties—birthdays, holidays, personal celebrations. Although for many years we were missionaries living in a foreign land with few creature comforts and less money, we never allowed pity to show its face around our home. In the red-light district the four of us lived in a tiny apartment much smaller than the average hotel room. We didn't obtain our first kitchen and private bathroom until we moved into a training center outside of Amsterdam, a full eight years after we were married!

For spiritual fun, we kept a prayer log of the things we prayed for as a family and carefully noted God's answers. It was an adventure in learning about honest prayer. Our kids learned what was appropriate to request, how to trust God, and celebrating and giving thanks when He answered their prayer.

Sally and I agreed that if we enjoyed life and were secure in its adventure, our kids would follow suit. And they did. They thought they had the best experience of everything. You see, *having fun doesn't depend on having money, but rather on an attitude of life!*

One person said long ago that children are homemade, and I'm convinced that fun is one of the most special things about homemade children! Anyone who wants it can have it.

## TAKING A DAY OFF

We learned at L'Abri to take a day off religiously. Dr. Schaeffer was not legalistic about anything *except* his staff taking a day off. He insisted on it. No one could work on his day off; he was to do something with his family. So from early on, Saturday was a special day for Sally and me. If I ministered on Saturday, Sunday was a day off. We went out and had fun someplace. Celebration was a part of our family commitment.

I believe this is both wise and biblical. Can you name the longest of the Ten Commandments? It's not, "You shall have no other gods before me" (Exodus 20:3), as I would have suspected. The longest is the fourth commandment—the instruction to "remember the Sabbath day by keeping it holy. Six days you shall labor and do all your work, but the seventh day is a Sabbath to the LORD your God" (Exodus 20:8-10). A quick read through the Old Testament will show you how angry God became when His people ignored this commandment. Apparently it is very dear to His heart.

But why? Why care so deeply about whether people observe a day of rest? I suppose there are many reasons, but I can think of two in particular. First, people were not created to work nonstop. God "rested" on the seventh day not because He was tired, but to give us a supreme example. If He rested, who are we to think we can skip rest? Second—and this is the more important of the two, I believe—the Sabbath is not so much a sabbath *for* us as it is *to* God. Exodus 20:10 says, "The seventh day is a Sabbath *to* the LORD your God" (emphasis added). God knows we tend to forget that we are *His* children. We need one day in the week to focus on Him, remember that we belong to Him, give thanks for His many blessings, and celebrate His goodness. We need a day of rest to remember who God is and who we are called to be.

But don't think for a moment that this is some sort of long-faced, dreary, duty-bound mandate that requires a clenched jaw and stiff upper lip. Hardly! This commandment, like all of God's commands, was given specifically "so that you may *enjoy* long life" (*see* Deuteronomy 6:2, emphasis added). You won't find the word "fun" in the Bible, but you will discover hundreds of references to terms such as "enjoy" and "delight" and "rejoice" and "pleasures" and "happy." You will find verses such as Psalm 2:11: "Serve the LORD with fear and rejoice with trembling." You will hear Jesus say things like, "Happy are those who long to be just and good, for they shall be completely satisfied" (Matthew 5:6 TLB). And one day, if you heed the Bible's instructions, you will hear the Lord Himself say, "Well done, good and faithful servant! You have been faithful with a few things; I will put you in charge of many things. Come and share your master's happiness!" (Matthew 25:21).

We dads must never forget that we serve a God who knows how to enjoy Himself. The Lord knows how to have a good time! What other kind of God could inspire one of His children to write, "You have made known to me the path of life; you will fill me with joy in your presence, with eternal pleasures at your right hand" (Psalm 16:11)?

## STAGES OF FUN

Some men find it possible to have fun with their kids at one stage of life, but not at others. One of our challenges is to have fun with our kids at every stage—when they are infants, when they are toddlers, when they are children, when they are teenagers, and when they become adults. Having fun with them allows us to get to know them in different ways at different stages of their lives. For simplicity's sake, I have broken down these stages of fun into five categories:

1. *Infancy.* We can help bathe our infants, get them ready for bed, get them dressed before we go to work,

and read to them. This is our opportunity to start developing patterns and habits that will carry through the rest of their lives. If we wait until our kids are two or three years old, it's too late to enjoy them as the curious, marvelous little creations they are. We can hold them, talk to them, tell them stories, and play with them.

You might consider getting a book or two on child development so you will be aware of what your child is seeing when he is 5, 15, and 25 days old, when he becomes self-aware, and what he is learning. Did you know that 95 percent of all the sounds that a child makes in his first six months are common to every language in the world? Eventually they retain only the sounds that they hear and repeat; the others die out. So even at this stage, there is no time to lose!

2. *Ages 9 months to 2 years.* Read books together, play on the floor, teach them to walk, play with a puppy or kitten, enjoy their toys, and tell stories. Children who discover in their first two years that learning is fun establish a pattern that remains for the rest of their lives. This is an age when kids are both fascinated with and afraid of animals, and it is a great time to introduce them to pets. Take them to the zoo and watch the marvelous looks of wonder on their faces.

3. *Ages 2 to 6 years.* Make up stories, read books, play outside, and toss a ball. I would sit down on the floor with my legs spread apart and roll a ball back and forth to my children. You can play on activity sets or swings, talk about what they play with, listen to their interests, take them out for special appointments, or get in the car and go to the restaurant for a cup of coffee and

ice cream. Go shopping, visit a park, walk around the neighborhood, drive out in the country, or go fishing.

4. *Ages 6 to 11 years.* Play sports together, coach, read biographies, tell stories, read joke books and cartoons, do hobbies and crafts together, go on hikes, fly kites, pull practical jokes, plan vacations, take them to work and explain what you do, enjoy special celebrations, watch videos about animals, and establish a once-a-week family night.

5. *Ages 12 to 17 years.* Attend movies together and discuss them, listen to pop music together and talk about it, play catch, tell jokes, and do activities that give your son or daughter the privilege of doing something that's normally associated with adulthood. For example, since Amsterdam was rainy and Matthew was not into soccer or any other European sports, we started going to pool halls. These weren't dirty places, but family-oriented billiards parlors where people played pool. Eventually we both became really good and had a blast together. I was trying to introduce my son to the real world and have fun at the same time.

Misha and I used to make appointments to go out for a cup of hot chocolate after school. We would go to a museum together, stay just 10-15 minutes, and as soon as she wanted to leave, we left. We did anything that was an adventure. If it was possible and not dangerous, we would do it.

6. *Grandkids.* Our own children are not yet married so we don't have grandkids, but I'm looking forward to the day when Sally and I will fill the shoes of grandparents. May the fun continue!

Dads, how much fun do we really have? I would like us to stop for a moment to discover where we fit on the following "Family Fun Quotient" scale. Rate yourself on a 1-5 scale in each of the categories listed below, with 1 meaning, "Baptized in pickle juice" and 5 meaning, "Could start his own circus." And please—don't take it so *seriously!*

### _____ Family Fun Quotient _____

- Make a list of fun things your kids would like to do. Ask them, "What would you like to do that you haven't yet done?"

  *1   2   3   4   5*

- Have backup plans in mind in case something falls through, like taking a tour of the local radio or TV station.

  *1   2   3   4   5*

- Plan vacations together—you set the budget and time parameters, but allow your kids to help set the agenda. And don't drive 600 miles a day to get someplace. Have fun!

  *1   2   3   4   5*

- Do things together with other families from your neighborhood or church. Have a picnic and play some ball together.

  *1   2   3   4   5*

- Check out the kids' organizations and programs in your city, such as the YMCA, library, school, or swimming pool, and participate in activities with them.

*1  2  3  4  5*

- Visit a dairy farm or horse farm. Arrange for the farmer or ranch manager to conduct a tour. Added point: Visit during the spring when calves or foals are born!

*1  2  3  4  5*

- See who can give the craziest, funniest card for the next birthday in your family. File the cards away and then bring them all out for each new birthday so you can laugh at them again.

*1  2  3  4  5*

- Buy a Bill Cosby tape or video and enjoy it as a family. Bill is fun and clean.

*1  2  3  4  5*

- Read a good book together. In fact, entice your children by reading a little bit each evening after supper for those in the family who want to stick around and enjoy the fun.

*1  2  3  4  5*

- Pull out all the old family photos you have stored in shoe boxes and get the whole family involved in organizing and putting them into albums. Laugh as you look!

*1  2  3  4  5*

How did you score? If your total was under 20, you need surgery to have a laugh bone implanted. Get with it, dad!

## BOTTOM LINE: HAVE FUN!

Did you know that the original Popsicle was invented by an 11-year-old? In 1905 little Frank Epperson wanted to do something fun for his friends. Those were the days before modern refrigerators, so he placed a stick in a jar of fruit juice, put it outside overnight, and it froze. Since that time, more than *70 billion* Popsicles have been ravenously consumed by kids around the world. And it all started with one little boy who was having fun.

Dads, if your kids have as much fun as Frank did, you might get to retire early. Didn't I tell you that fun could be profitable?

## _____ *ACTION STEPS* _____

Are you a fun dad? Pick an item from the "Family Fun Quotient" list... or, select one or more of the following suggested activities to do with your family this week. Better yet, try to do all of the below within one month!

• Go to a school or professional ball game.

• Set up a tent in the backyard and let the kids "camp out" overnight.

- Go stargazing one evening, and try to identify as many constellations as you can.

- Go to three garage sales one weekend.

- Help your kids write letters of appreciation to their mom...and mail them!

- Take a scenic drive to a destination at least an hour away from home, and eat out at a restaurant you have never gone to before.

# 9

# Don't Check
# Your Brain
# at the Door

I love to go for walks with my dog, Mack, a choco-late-colored Labrador. He weighs about 90 pounds, is full of energy, and is strong-willed. He loves to play and wrestle. I look forward to our walks not only for the exercise they afford me but also as a time to meditate and pray.

We live in the country and the road in front of our house ends close to a national forest. On a recent Sunday I walked out the driveway from my house and turned away from the forest to walk down the road when out of nowhere a pack of dogs rushed at me, snarling, teeth bared, and barking. There must have been half a dozen or more of them, strange-looking dogs, a mixture of gray-brown-black-white. They reminded me of Australian cattle dogs.

Mack was startled so I commanded him to sit and stay while I ran out toward the dogs to try chasing them away. It didn't work. They kept coming, and now they were coming after *me*. My heart pounded.

I grabbed rocks to throw at the dogs, but slipped and fell. Two dogs lunged toward me, nipping at my face and legs. I jumped up and tried to grab something to throw at the pack to make it retreat. Just then I heard a voice down the street—the owner of the dogs, commanding them to come. A little old lady was out for a morning stroll with her pack of canine teeth!

Keep that picture in mind as I tell you another story, this one also true. A survey taken 50 years ago asked high school teachers to name the three greatest problems students presented in their schools. Their answers: 1) chewing gum in class; 2) running in the hallway; 3) talking back to the teacher. Recently the survey was taken again, but the results were startlingly different. This time the answers were: 1) guns and knives; 2) drugs and alcohol; 3) rape and teenage pregnancy.

*Our kids face pressures and temptations that we can scarcely imagine.*

I think a lot of kids today feel as I did when the pack of dogs attacked me. They feel overwhelmed. They are surrounded. They are being nipped at, bitten, threatened, and growled at. In the same way that I slipped on the gravel and fell, kids are falling today—and it's not hard to understand why.

Our kids face pressures and temptations that we can scarcely imagine. We might wish for a world in which there was no television, pop music, MTV, theaters, drugs, bombardment of nonbiblical religions or philosophies of life, or challenge to the truth of God—but that's not the real world. We might wish for such a culture, but we are not likely to get it. The truth is, we are in a tremendous battle for our kids.

## GOD UNDER ATTACK

Every aspect of the nature and character of God is under assault today. Through radio music and talk shows, on television movies and MTV, in magazines and books and even in school, it is assumed that there is no God. The existence of God is denied—or if there is a God, it's certain He is not an infinite, personal being. He is an impersonal force or a spirit-guide. In fact, "He" is not even a *he*. It is a spirit that lives in all of us. We are told that we're all gods!

The self-existence of God is under attack. People teach and believe that the universe either always has been or somehow came into existence on its own. The power of God is under attack, especially by those embittered with the problems of world suffering. Non-Christians want the best of both worlds: They blame God when they need a scapegoat, but disbelieve in Him the rest of the time.

The majesty and wisdom of God are also under attack. People refuse to submit to His lordship, they reject His authority, and believe that He is not a good God. His holiness is brought into question because people growing up in this depraved society have no comprehension of what holiness might look like. As to the love of God, what does love mean in this Hollywood-infected Babylon of ours?

God as Spirit is under attack through the mystical religions and the New Age thinking of Shirley Mac-Laine and her cohorts. People no longer believe God is truth because our society rejects absolute truth. There are only two truths in this society: We are free, and we should have fun. That is why Tolerance is the god of the age. That is why Christians are hated so ferociously—we are the ones who believe in a moral God, a God of truth, a God who is personal and who wants to be involved in our lives, and a God who is infinite and therefore rules over our lives. Such beliefs constitute a grave threat to the two great values of Freedom and Fun.

## WE ARE, THEREFORE WE MUST THINK

If ever there were a generation that needed to be taught to think both biblically and critically, it is this one. A thousand mind-rotting and body-wasting philosophies are offered for sale at every street corner in the land, and kids who don't know how to think biblically are almost certainly doomed to buy the poison. If we do not protect our children and teach them to understand truth and to think critically from a biblical perspective, we are sending them out to play on a street menaced by a pack of snarling, vicious, rabies-infected dogs.

None of us as parents want to do that. I know I don't, and I'm sure you don't, either—that's why you are reading this chapter. It is essential that we teach our children to think. The key questions we must ask over and over again about everything are, "Is it *true*? Is what's being said *trustworthy*? Is what people believe *correct*?" Don't merely ask, "Is it true for you?" Rather, ask, "Is it true in the absolute sense that it is eternal and unchangeable? Does it come out of the heart of our unchanging God? Is it consistent with that which God has revealed about Himself?"

## A TOUGH CHALLENGE

The challenge before us as men today is the same one given by God to fathers in the book of Deuteronomy. After instructing them to "fear the LORD your God as long as you live" (Deuteronomy 6:2) and to obey His commands (verse 3), God says through Moses:

> Love the LORD your God with all your heart and with all your soul and with all your strength. These commandments that I give you today are to be upon your hearts. Impress them on your children. Talk about them when you sit at home and when you walk along the road, when you lie down and when you get up.
>
> —*Deuteronomy 6:5-7*

Fathers in Moses' day were specifically given the duty of teaching their children to think about the law of

God. They were to teach them in the streets, at the gates, at home, in the morning, and at night. In other words, this is not the Sunday School teacher's job, which comprises about one hour a week.

Not only were the fathers to teach their children the truth all week long, but it was also their responsibility to convey the *spirit* of truth. It is possible to have an informed mind but an infidel's heart. That is what the Lord meant when through Isaiah he said of Israel, "These people come near to me with their mouth and honor me with their lips, but their hearts are far from me. Their worship of me is made up only of rules taught by men" (Isaiah 29:13).

The letter of the truth alone—merely repeating words spoken about God without living in a way that embodies that truth—actually does more harm than good. Truth must come not just from the mind, but also from the heart. God is not pleased with mere theoretical acquaintance with biblical truth; it must be experienced relationally with God. Our goal should not be to pass along theory from one mind to another, but to rear boys and girls who are committed to the God behind the theory. We must first understand and live out the truth of who God is—His nature and His character—for ourselves, and then pass along that kind of knowledge from our own heart and mind to the hearts and minds of our children and family.

Truth is relationship-based. Everything that God does is motivated by relationship. Truth without relationship is oppressive law and bondage. Truth without relationship cannot transform anyone into the image of Christ; in fact, it often mutates them into creatures on

the opposite end of the righteousness scale. It is therefore no wonder that Isaiah put the concept of relationship squarely at the center of his thoughts concerning
God: "He will be the sure foundation for your times, a
rich store of salvation and wisdom and knowledge; the
fear of the LORD is the key to this treasure" (Isaiah
33:6).

The prophet pictures knowledge and wisdom and
salvation as priceless treasures locked up securely in
heaven's storehouse. This is wealth and riches beyond
imagination—but it is absolutely unavailable to anyone
without the proper key. And what is the key? Only one
in all the universe fits the lock: "the fear of the LORD"
is the key to this treasure. The key, Isaiah tells us, is
an intimate, rich, growing relationship with the Lord.
Only those who fear God—who revere Him for who He
is and what He has done—can ever enter the heavenly
vault and gorge themselves on its treasures of knowledge, wisdom, and salvation.

Men, this is a nonnegotiable. This is to be a way of
life for every man. Seeking God and leading our kids
into truth is a responsibility He puts squarely on the
shoulders of every man. If you are failing in this responsibility, then I urge you to ask God to forgive you and to
get on with the job. Don't go into a fit of depression—
just confess your failure to God, ask His forgiveness,
and then take up the suggestions offered in this book.
Teach your family to love truth and seek God's wisdom!

## WHAT SHOULD WE THINK ABOUT?

Scripture exhorts us "whatever is true, whatever is
noble, whatever is right, whatever is pure, whatever is

lovely, whatever is admirable—if anything is excellent or praiseworthy—think about such things" (Philippians 4:8). And I can't think of anything that meets those criteria better than the nature and character of God. In an era that attacks everything God is and stands for, I believe we must find ways to talk frequently with our children about God as He has revealed Himself in the Bible and through Jesus Christ. There are ten aspects of the nature and character of God that I believe are essential for every Christian to consider and understand.

1. God is infinite.

2. God is self-existent.

3. God is all-powerful.

4. God is spirit.

5. God is truth.

6. God is unchanging.

7. God is majestic.

8. God is wise.

9. God is holy.

10. God is love.

I don't want to take time now to develop each of these great themes—monumental books have been written about each one!—but I do want to give you someplace to start. In the first chapter of my book *Finding Friendship with God* (Vine Books, 1993), I give a brief overview of each of these ten truths. You might want to start there if this is new territory for you. You can also begin your own study of each of these great Bible truths. I suggest you keep a notebook and write down verses or passages of Scripture that relate to each of these themes about God's nature and character.

## THREE ARENAS FOR INSTRUCTION

The passage in Deuteronomy 6 suggests at least three spheres of life in which we can teach our children about the truth of God. All three should be used for greatest effectiveness, and all three share one thing in common: the power of interaction (discussion and asking questions), which is key to learning.

1. *Actual teaching.* One of the best ways to explain things is through family devotions by reading and explaining God's Word to our children from the time they are infants. You could read through the Gospels and explain them as you go. Try to focus on the basic nature and character of God. Be sure to ask questions to see if your children are following you. Lay a foundation for their future, when they will acquire a more adult understanding.

2. *Family experiences.* Use holidays, celebrations, symbols, rituals, traditions, and memorials to celebrate the truths of who God is. These might include the events or natural experiences that come up or the traditions we build around Easter, Christmas, and each Sunday.

Ruth Bell Graham, wife of evangelist Billy Graham,

has said that on Sundays her family always did something special with the children. They were not allowed to eat sweets or ice cream Monday through Saturday, but on Sunday they could because Sunday was a special day and the Grahams wanted their children to have a positive view of God's character. On Sunday they always did something extra to celebrate. Often these times were built around meals or some family experience. Ruth and Billy wanted to teach their children about God's character—that He is a good God, a loving God, a God of relationship, and a personal God.

> *Relationships allow us to use the problems of life to teach our kids godly principles and precepts.*

When Sally and I got married, I opposed most Christmas and Easter traditions. I was young and idealistic and I wanted to get to the true meaning of Christmas and Easter. But my wife loved trimming trees and hanging up lights and ornaments and setting out special holiday decorations. Eventually I figured out that in my desire to get to the truth, I was missing the truth. I was missing an important tradition that God wanted to give our family—a tradition that would communicate the character of God. Now Christmas is my favorite time of the year. We have built many wonderful memories around our family Christmases.

3. *Relationships.* Relationships allow us to use the interruptions, tragedies, conflicts, and problems of life to teach our kids godly principles and precepts. Their fights with friends and challenges at school and work provide a fertile forum for discussing what God expects of His children. Out of this, we teach.

## SIX STEPS TO THINKING

Dr. Benjamin Bloom has developed a six-step model for learning that I think is both excellent and simple. I have used it in my own home with some success, and I hope it benefits you in the same way it did me.

1. *Give information and help your children recall it through repetition and memorization.* Talk about something with your kids over a meal and then ask them the next day, "What did you think about that?" Get them to repeat the information.

2. *Help your children understand the truth by restating it in their own words.* If you are teaching your children about the importance of forgiveness, first ask them to repeat what you said, then ask them to explain what that means in their own words.

3. *Teach your children to apply the truth.* "OK, what did we say about this? What was it?" After your children repeat the information, you could say, "Now, how does that work in this situation?" Give them a real-life situation where they need to think about how to *apply* what they have learned. As they apply it to their own life, they are truly learning to think biblically.

4. *Teach your children to analyze the truth.* Try to get them to derive principles and to project them theoretically into other situations. Children between the ages of 2-10 will think more concretely, but around age 11 or 12 they begin to make the transition to more conceptual thinking.

5. *Teach your children to synthesize the truth.* Here they combine the various principles they have analyzed individually. We teach them to look at implications or conclusions. For example: If Muslims believe that Jesus did not die on the cross, what is the implication? They must combine an item of fact (that Jesus *did* die on the cross) with another fact (Muslims teach that He did not), and make conclusions. What does that mean about Islam? I believe that parents should expose their children to the world religions, especially after they reach the age of 11 or 12, when they are starting to think more theoretically and conceptually. We get them to draw conclusions and implications not on the basis of a religion's doctrine, but on the basis of biblical truth.

6. *Teach your children to evaluate the truth.* In this final step they put everything together and make judgments and set values. Evaluation is the stage of determining and fixing one's values and philosophy of life based on drawing together those principles already learned. This is a natural step, and comes as a result of going through the other five steps outlined above.

## TWO KEY QUESTIONS

It's one thing to digest true information about God;

it's another to use that knowledge in day-to-day living situations. How do we apply our knowledge about the nature and character of God to every aspect of our lives—to every problem that we face?

I would like to present a simple grid that I have found useful in teaching my own children to think critically and biblically. Without exception, every question that our family faces in life comes back to one or two questions:

1. The question of being: Why are we here? How did we get here?

2. The question of morality: What is right? What should we do?

All questions in life come back to one of these two. We could call these the questions of personality and morality. We do not need four Ph.D. degrees to challenge the different philosophies that our kids come up against. We don't have to be university-educated to be smart. There are many educated men and women in our world who are able to regurgitate volumes of information, but who are also fools in God's eyes. So don't be intimidated by the so-called "smart" people.

God wants us to interpret the world to the worldly. In order to do that, we apply the questions about personality and morality. A father who understands how to answer the questions that come up in these two key areas will be a wise man. He will be smarter than the worldly philosophers and the liberal theologians. He will be smarter than the religious gurus and self-appointed intellectuals. Why? Because he will stand on the basis of truth from God's perspective and be able to point out the inconsistencies, loopholes, and nonsense that people often propose as truth.

You don't have to understand the theory of atheistic evolution, for example, to be able to help your children think through its flaws and fallacies. Apply the question of personality to it. I have asked my kids, "What are the possible answers to the basic question of existence? Either we came from chance, or we came from design. Either there was an infinite, personal God who created us, or we came from slime plus time plus chance. If we came from the latter, we have to face the logical conclusions. If we are merely the product of chance, then all the aspirations we have for meaning— all our longings for love, relationship, and adventure— are meaningless. If atheistic evolution is true, then we are just highly developed snails. We may think we have meaning, but we don't because we are only here by chance. Try to live like that!"

A father can point this out to his children. He can say, "Either we are here because there was a design for us and therefore we have significance, or we are just highly developed animals. If we are accidents of nature, then love doesn't have meaning because it is simply a series of biological impulses. It's nothing more than reproductive drives—just biology and chemistry. On the other hand, if we are created in the image of a personal, infinite God, then relationships can and do have tremendous significance and meaning. We are not here by chance, but to fulfill a purpose designed for us by a loving Creator."

Or, think of the second question—the one of morality. Our I.Q. doesn't have to be off the scale to be able to see through the moral fallacies of atheistic evolution. Either there is a God who gave us laws to live by, or there is no God and therefore no morality—no right and wrong. People can say there is right and wrong; they can feel there is right and wrong; but if they insist there is no God, they should admit that morality disappears. All that is left is preferences and men deciding for themselves what is right and wrong. Try to live like that! One man's "right" is another's "wrong," and who is to decide between them? You might prefer that I not kill your dog, but if there is no God and thus there are no absolutes, why shouldn't I lace his food with cyanide if I don't like his barking?

A world without God is a violent and selfish place. We can point out to our children that people should be confronted with the logical conclusions of their choices.

## ASKING QUESTIONS

To find out what people believe, we can ask the *what* questions: "What do you mean by that? What do you *not* mean by that?" Then we can ask: "What are the logical conclusions of what you believe?" If someone says there is no God, we can focus on the question of personality. If there is no God, then our life really doesn't have meaning. Suicide doesn't matter, and neither does war. And if that is true, then why do we punish criminals? Aren't they merely living out what instinct tells them to do? And if so, why should we punish them or try to reform them?

We can also ask the *why* questions: "Why do you believe that? Why do you believe it is wrong to do that?"

This often helps to expose inconsistencies. "Why do you believe it is wrong to murder if you don't believe in a God? Why do you believe that relationships have meaning if there is no God?"

> *The best place to teach our kids to think is in the messiness of everyday living.*

We should get people to define the words they use because, in our world, many words no longer carry the same meaning they once did. So if someone talks about "God," we can ask, "What do you mean when you say, 'God'? What is the logical conclusion if you say there is a God, but He is not personal?" Asking these kinds of questions is a matter of thinking, not just memorizing facts.

## FROM FEELING TO FACTS

Another way to help our children learn to think is to realize that people often think best when they move from the subjective to the objective—from feelings to facts. We are created in the image of God with the ability to feel, and we often react emotionally to something before we understand it intellectually. In the learning process, it is important to let people express their emotional reaction before we go on to observe what they are reacting to, why they are reacting, and what they can learn from it. We should not shut down the subjective, but use it as a stepping-stone to the objective.

Most of us learn best by moving from feelings to meaning. We need to verbalize emotions in order to understand why we feel those emotions. If a child is going through a hard time, a father can lead him or her to understanding by asking four questions: 1) "How are you feeling?" 2) "What did you experience that led to those feelings?" 3) "What lessons or principles did you learn from this?" 4) "What now?"

This last step is where we lead our kids into right responses: "Let's pray and forgive Joey for what he said. Do you think we should go and talk to Joey and his parents together?" Be prepared to back up your words with actions!

## TEST CASE: THE HOME

The best place to teach our kids to think is in the messiness of everyday living. Over the years Sally and I have enjoyed many opportunities to test what I have written in this chapter, but one of the most effective episodes was also one of the most difficult.

When Matthew and Misha were about 13 and 15, we told them, "You can listen to any Christian music that we discuss together. We want to know what it says and how it feels to you, but you can choose your own music as long as it is Christian." It wasn't a rule so much as it was just something I wanted. But a crisis arose when they started sneaking in non-Christian rock music on the radio and on MTV, which had just come to Europe.

Once I realized what was happening, I raised the issue with them. Still, I didn't say no to non-Christian music. I did, however, tell them I was concerned about how it was affecting their attitudes. I wanted them to think through the implications of what they were listening to and how it was affecting our household. I wanted them to ask the question about morality, about right and wrong. I wanted them to think for themselves, not merely comply with a rule.

But as the weeks went by it hit me that I was no longer the priest in my own home and that Sally and I no longer set the spiritual tone for our family. Immediately I decided that I was not going to vacate that role of leadership and influence. After fasting and praying, I sat the kids down one night and said, "It's clear to me that I'm no longer setting the spiritual tone for this family. Music is your constant diet and your mother and I are no longer the pacesetters in this family. That's unacceptable to me. This is not a negotiable. You may enter into dialogue with me about *how* changes are made, but changes *must* be made."

My goal was to get my children engaged in owning this decision. We talked over several things, music being the predominant issue. I said to them, "I'm not happy with the influence of your music. I have tried to be open, to set the pace, and to say I think God has created all kinds of music. I gave you six or seven principles for discerning whether music was godly or ungodly, but you haven't been using them." When they saw where this discussion was heading, they quickly polarized.

So I just said, "I'm sorry, but no non-Christian music in the house, period. And no Christian artist that I think is ungodly. No radio, no MTV, nothing. This is it. I'll cancel every speaking engagement I have to stay here and censor your every waking hour if necessary. I will do it because this is not about music, this is about who sets the tone in this home. And I will not surrender that. If you don't want to live here—if you say this is unfair—OK, I'll help you find someplace else to live. But I am not surrendering this."

Please understand that I don't judge the godliness of music on the basis of how loud it is. The problem was *not* solely about music. I think that's where many parents make a mistake. They pass a rule against music and fail to deal with the heart. To me, *this* was a heart issue.

For about two weeks there was strong tension in the home. I'm sure you can identify with what I'm talking about. Every man I have talked to who has teenagers has faced the same challenge. When it happened to us, I was praying like crazy—and thank God, Misha was the first to have a breakthrough. God convicted her that I was right because I related the issue to attitude and spirit. She apologized and said, "You're right, Dad. God has shown me that I was not following your lead; I was following another lead. And it was affecting my spirit." She went back and forth on that conviction, but for her it became a spiritual milestone. Matthew eventually followed suit.

Now that you know the story, let me say to you man to man how difficult I have found the challenge of helping my kids to deal with rock music. This challenge in my home was not easy to master. Nor is it easy to handle all the other challenges we face in raising good kids. But I want to encourage you to believe that God will guide us if we humble ourselves and cry out to Him for wisdom. In many arenas of life, we men are deeply affecting our children's future. It's going to take time and sacrifice and a willingness on our part to seek God on these difficult matters. There are no easy solutions, especially when it comes to the issue of rock-and-roll music.

## HOW HIGH ARE THOSE THOUGHTS?

Teaching our kids to think for themselves along biblical lines is a challenging, tiring, and sometimes draining process, but it is one of the nonnegotiables of the Christian life. If we don't think, we are going to get run over by the devil. If we don't use our minds to wrestle with the tough issues, we are going to compromise and we won't even know it. I have concluded that we can't survive in this world unless we stretch ourselves to think through the hard issues. But if we do it and we are willing to pay the price, the rewards are enormous!

The world out there is a ferocious place, far more dangerous than any jungle I know of. If we want our kids to survive and even thrive on the mean streets of this planet, we must teach them to think: to think biblically; to think critically; and most of all, to think of the One who says,

> Seek the LORD while he may be found;
>   call on him while he is near.
>
> Let the wicked forsake his way
>   and the evil man his thoughts.
>
> Let him turn to the LORD, and he will
>     have mercy on him,
>   and to our God, for he will freely
>     pardon.

"For my thoughts are not your thoughts,
neither are your ways my ways,"
declares the LORD.

As the heavens are higher than the
earth, so are my ways higher than
your ways, and my thoughts than
your thoughts.

—*Isaiah 55:6-9*

# _____ *ACTION STEPS* _____

- The best kind of preventative medicine for protecting your kids from ungodly influences is to impart God's truth and practical wisdom to them. Have you made this a priority in your life? Don't let busyness be an excuse...even mealtime can be used to provide your children with biblical perspectives. Think of a timely issue you can discuss with your family during the next meal. Ask for your children's input, and dialogue together. Next, do this twice in one week...then three times. Try to work toward encouraging such interaction frequently.

- Do you pray for each of your children daily? That's a nonnegotiable desperately needed in today's society. Cultivate a habit of lifting your children up to God daily, or even throughout the day. And don't be general; be *specific*. Pray for the battles they face at school or among their peers. Ask God to give them wisdom and to allow you opportunity to equip your children to handle their problems in a godly way.

- Is there a prime-time TV show that you feel portrays inappropriate family values? Write a letter to the network and share your concerns.

- Unplug the TV, radio, stereo, CD player (or whatever) for one full evening, and spend time in genuine interaction with your family. Make a commitment to doing this at least once a week!

# 10

# Believing God for the Impossible

I recently read about a pilot from Titusville, Florida, who for years had been at work restoring an antique airplane. One afternoon he decided to take his vintage biplane out for a flight. He had no one to help him, however, so he went out on the tarmac alone, got his airplane carefully positioned on the runway, ran to the nose of the aircraft, spun the propeller, then ran back to hop into the cockpit. After the engine sputtered to life and began to idle, the pilot had to jump out again to kick out the blocks from under the tires.

Just before he was able to climb back in, the aircraft bolted forward and started careening down the runway without him. The plane gained speed, took off, and was airborne. That was the last this poor, hapless pilot saw of his airplane as it wobbled out to sea and crashed.

> *If we don't have faith in*
> *God, our kids won't either.*

This story reminds me of the labor—and sometimes, the tragic labor—of parents pouring their lives into preparing their children for adulthood. Yet their children head out into life without any real sense of direction and quickly crash. For us as men, this means that our parenting energy needs to be focused, controlled, and planned. It's not enough to say, "I'm going to raise my kids to be good kids." We must train our children in such a way that they can fly with clear direction and skill.

The challenge for us is to impart to them a faith in God—one of the most important nonnegotiables of all. If we don't have faith in God, our kids won't either, and if they don't have faith in God, they will be overcome by evil.

In order to help our sons and daughters develop a real, living, adventuresome, solid, biblically based, radical faith in God, we ourselves must be people of faith. We must have some idea of what we want our kids to turn out like. Failure to focus our own spiritual walk means we won't be able to build their spirituality on strong, biblical foundations.

This is part of passing on the nonnegotiables—the biblical principles we live by—to our children, even as they grow into adulthood. My burning desire has been to be a man of integrity, a principled man. I have longed to pass on these nonnegotiable values to my children. I want them to think biblically, to celebrate life and have fun, to trust God, fear the Lord, and to be strong, warm, and involved in the lives of people. I know this won't happen by accident—therefore, this book.

In this final chapter, I want to share some lessons I have learned about how we might pass on to our children a vibrant faith in the living God. I want to zero in on trusting God for the impossible—on believing in God to do great things through us. In other words, how do we foster in our family a radical faith in God?

## WILL THE REAL DISCIPLES PLEASE STAND UP?

The following is a concise list of characteristics found in true disciples.[1] If you were to rate each of them in order of importance, in what order would you place them?

- Careful student of the Scriptures
- Zealous and active for God
- Active in worship and prayer
- Consistent in worship attendance
- Memorizes Scripture
- Unafraid to pray publicly
- Active in the affairs of the local congregation
- Fasts regularly
- Stands against unrighteousness
- Understands foundational theological truths

What does your list look like? By the way, I suppose I should tell you I forgot to mention that all these items have one factor in common: They are all traits and behaviors characteristic not of Jesus' disciples, but of the Pharisees!

Isn't it ironic that the traits we most often identify with real, on-fire, enthusiastic followers of Jesus are frequently the very traits that we often don't see in the lives of people who really *are* godly? We tend to focus on outward behavior rather than on the heart. If someone's list of religious activities is long, we tend to think he must be doing well. As long as nobody labels him a Pharisee, he looks pretty godly to us. But it may just be that we are missing the point.

## WHAT IS FAITH?

What does it *really* mean to have faith in God? And why is it such an important nonnegotiable?

Real faith is not frequent attendance at meetings, but what our lives exhibit between meetings. Real faith is not so much the number of Scriptures we memorize, but understanding and living by the scriptural principles we do know. Real faith does not mean we are busy at church every night and twice on Sunday, but that we have fellowship with a body of Christians to whom we are accountable. Real faith does not so much mean we fast every week, but that we are *not afraid of nor unaccustomed to* fasting as a means of drawing closer to God.

I believe Ephesians 1:17-19 and 4:11-16 suggest four elements of the kind of faith that will help us to build strong families. Remember: Real and growing faith has little to do with a laundry list of religious activities.

1. *Faith is Christ-centered* (Ephesians 1:17-19). Real faith is more concerned about teaching our children how much Jesus loves them, how good He is, and what He has done for them rather than with getting them to memorize a list of dos and don'ts!

Faith starts with the revelation to our hearts that we are loved by God—and that He dwells in us. A heart of faith responds out of thankfulness and gratefulness, not out of cold obedience to a set of rules. Inward awareness that Christ loves us and dwells within us is the fruit of faith, not compliance with accepted behaviors. In Ephesians 1:17-19 Paul asks that God "may give you a spirit of wisdom and revelation in the knowledge of him, having the eyes of your hearts enlightened, that you may know . . . what is the immeasurable greatness of his power in us *who believe*" (RSV, emphasis added).

Too much of modern Western theology is sin-oriented and man-centered rather than grace-rooted and God-focused. Instead of emphasizing who God is in us and confessing His character and letting Him become greater to us than our circumstances, we have lingered over our own impoverished abilities and our sin and weaknesses and failures. We tend to forget that nothing is too hard for God (*see* Jeremiah 32:27), whether it's what He wants to do *in* us or what He wants to do *through* us.

2. *Faith is world-engaging* (Ephesians 4:12). By reading the newspaper with our kids, talking over current

events, discussing the problems of world famine, and taking our kids with us to respond to such problems— whether on a short-term missions trip to Mexico, by getting involved in an inner-city outreach, by building relationships with the poor, or by otherwise caring and responding to the world's pain—we are preparing them for works of service. That's what Ephesians 4:12 instructs leaders to do: "to prepare God's people for works of service, so that the body of Christ may be built up." Our children will catch this commitment only if we are modeling it. They won't get it if we merely talk about it.

> *The fewer* activities *we are involved with and the more time we spend with people, the stronger our* relationships *will be.*

I once took Misha with me on an evangelistic trip just outside of London, where I spoke at a tent campaign sponsored by 115 English churches. I have taken my children with me to youth retreats where I was ministering to other kids. Sally and I have taken them with us to live in tents outside of Venice, Italy, where we went door to door and preached on the streets. We have taken them with us to witness to prostitutes and drug addicts in the streets of Amsterdam.

Don't think for a minute, however, that it is only missionaries who can provide their kids with such opportunities. I know of whole families who make an appointment each Thanksgiving to serve dinner at the local rescue mission, and others who volunteer each Christmas to deliver boxed goodies to poor families and migrant workers in their area. Some volunteer to teach English as a second language; others work with groups such as Habitat for Humanity, refurbishing older homes for families who otherwise would never be able to own one. If you truly want to show your kids that real faith is world-engaging, there are plenty of opportunities to do so—wherever you live!

3. *Faith is relationship-oriented* (Ephesians 4:16). Everything God does is based on relationship. He created people in His image for relationship with Himself. He sent Jesus to reconcile us to Himself, and it is His desire that we follow His example by developing relationships with others.

The fewer *activities* we are involved with and the more time we spend with people, the stronger our *relationships* will be. As we increase the number of our activities, we diminish our ability for personal involvement with people. If we reemphasize relationship, people will be more involved in our lives, they will remember more of what we are sharing, and they will capture more of our faith-shaped values.

As men, we have a unique opportunity to focus on our families and on a few other vital relationships. I don't mean we should sit around and hold hands, but I do mean that if we make it apparent that our kids are important to us, there is no way any of them will miss our commitment.

Ephesians 4:16 says the body of Christ "grows and builds itself up in love" by being "joined and held together by every supporting ligament...as each part does its work." This principle is not just for the church as a whole; it starts in our family. It is faith that allows us to support one another and be joined together in love. Faith starts in a family, not in a vacuum. Faith grows in a healthy environment of growing relationships.

4. *Faith is future-oriented and hope-producing* (Ephesians 4:13). Because our lives are in Christ and He is in us, we have the assurance that He will bring us to that place of maturity described in verse 13: "until we all reach unity in the faith and in the knowledge of the Son of God and become mature, attaining to the whole measure of the fullness of Christ."

God has a future and a hope for us, both in who we are and in what He is doing through us. He has a destiny for us! He has something special for us! He has gifts for us! Paul says in Ephesians 4:8 that Jesus "gave gifts to men." He has given gifts to our children and therefore we need to create an environment for those gifts to flourish. As we encourage our kids to trust Jesus and to do radical things for God, those gifts will come out. It's our job to create an atmosphere of trust in which we are constantly asking, "What is it that God wants us to trust Him for now? What kind of situation has He let us get into that requires us to believe Him for the impossible?" Such a practice gives kids a chance to prove God and to see how great He is.

This was true for my daughter when she was 12 years old and wanted to join a traveling evangelism group called the King's Kids. She didn't have the money to go on the trip, and neither did we. But we believed that if God wanted her to go with the King's Kids, He would make a way. So we said, "Misha, you do the possible; God will do the impossible. Let's believe God as a family for this money." As we prayed, sold things, and saved our money, God performed miracles for Misha. The money came in, and she went.

I remember when seven-year-old Matthew wanted to make a two-dollar-a-month pledge to a missions project. He didn't have the money, and we didn't think we should just give it to him. We believed this should be a prayer project for him and that he should have a part in seeing the money come in. So we said to him, "Why don't you collect things that people haven't been using and sell them?" He loved the idea and began collecting pencils, notepads, all kinds of items. Then he would put them on a tray and go from desk to desk and office to office at our YWAM headquarters, selling back to the people the very items they had donated! He fulfilled his pledge for two years, always coming up with new ideas for selling things. God also provided for him miraculously; people who had never before sent him money did so. Grandparents started sending checks at just the right time to meet the need. And his faith grew.

That is faith. It is faith that gives us a future and a hope. It was faith, working in tandem with the fear of God, that prompted Noah to build the ark and thereby save his family from annihilation: "By faith Noah, when warned about things not yet seen, in holy fear built an ark to save his family. By his faith he condemned the world and became heir of the righteousness that comes by faith" (Hebrews 11:7).

Faith looks out toward the horizon at a future it can't yet see and acts on God's promises. It steps out not into a dark void, but into the blazing presence of God, which blinds all other senses but faith.

Dads, we can play a vital role in encouraging our kids to believe God. It is our privilege to stand with them as we give counsel and advice. As we energetically partner with them in this adventure of faith, together we will see more clearly than ever the infinite faithfulness of God.

## STAGES OF FAITH

Everyone goes through stages in the development of their faith. A passage in 1 John lists three such stages: "children," "young men," and "fathers" (*see* 1 John 2:12-14). That everyone is not at the same stage should not alarm us. As we become aware of the various stages we go through in the growth of our faith, we will begin to notice that our children go through them as well. I believe everyone goes through certain, natural stages as their faith grows.

*First stage: Imitative faith.* This is the faith of children who are getting to know God. We imitate the faith we see in people around us. They inspire us, they are our heroes, they are models for us. Our parents often fill this role. On the other hand, if our parents have not had a vibrant faith, our own faith can suffer. We see that their faith meant little to them, and so ours may mean less to us. Studies have shown that the most on-fire Christians come either from the homes of dedicated, faithful Christian parents or from non-Christian families. Moms and dads with a lukewarm faith produce children who are either apathetic or cold toward God.

*Second stage: Fighting faith.* At this stage of belief in God, we know He is great and good and we dream of doing great things for Him, but we are not yet able to discern our God-given limitations. We dream big dreams about what God can do through us and what will happen in our life as a result of trusting Him. This stage of faith is described in 1 John 2:14 as producing strength to "overcome the evil one." This is faith to fight the devil and believe God for the victory.

Through the years, this kind of faith inevitably gets tested. People make all kinds of commitments and promises out of fighting faith. But eventually, experience tends to make clearer God's will and purpose for them. We should not discourage our children in their enthusiasm, but by our support and encouragement we should help them grow into a place where their faith is founded on God's character and His defeat of Satan.

There is a tremendous amount of inconsistency in faith at this stage because people can be red-hot when they have won a spiritual battle and ice-cold when they have been defeated. My own faith as a teenager was certainly up and down. One moment I was zealous for God, fighting the devil, and doing great exploits for God, and the next moment I was trying to get the victory over fighting my sister about whose turn it was to wash the dishes!

*Third stage: The faith of a father.* This person's faith has been tested and he is broken of the need to fight the devil. Instead, he has come into a personal, mature faith in God. Much testing precedes this stage: Will we put God first in our life? Will we stand up for Him under criticism? Will we step out and believe Him for things that seem impossible? Will we be faithful to Him in hard times? Faith that reaches this stage is rooted in the love of God.

Kids go through a unique transition when they leave the concrete thinking of adolescence and begin to think more abstractly and independently as teens. This is a challenging time for parents, but I think we should encourage them to test out their faith. If we have established a solid biblical foundation in the home and have nurtured a real friendship with our kids, we can view their steps of faith in a positive light. After all, if God is real, we already know those tests are going to reveal His faithfulness.

## CULTIVATING BIBLICAL VALUES

There are a host of ways to cultivate positive spiritual values in our kids.[2] I would like to spend just a few moments to discuss ten practical ideas, all of them related to faith.

1. *Don't hesitate to express your own faith.* Children need to know what we believe. We have a lot of competition from ungodly philosophies expressed through music, television, movies, and friends, and we need to express our faith in a positive, open, secure manner.

The primary responsibility for helping children to develop faith and form moral judgments falls to their parents, not the school or the church.

Even Dr. Benjamin Spock says, "The happiest and most successful youngsters are those whose parents present their beliefs unequivocally and expect their children to live up to them."

2. *Reinforce the faith that your children do have.* My dad and mom encouraged me in my faith all the time. They affirmed me when I read the Word and expressed spiritual hunger. They pointed out the positive aspects of my relationship with God. "I can see you have a hunger to learn," they would say. "You ask good questions, and I think God is happy with that." Or, "You are really faithful; I know that you are going to do great things for the Lord." They did this constantly.

3. *Live the kind of faith you want your child to have.* Children learn far better from example than from words alone. They catch a hunger for God far more readily through relationship than through mere theory. They need faith demonstrated so they can see its reality. Our faith becomes especially apparent as we spend time praying with our children.

*Kids are imitators, and it's great when they imitate genuine faith!*

When my kids were young, I would get up early in the morning and have my quiet time. Misha and Matthew would sit in my lap as I read the Bible. When I went for a walk to pray and meditate, I often took Matthew with me. We would go walking through the forest or around the city, and I would walk with my hands behind me, thinking and meditating. Sometimes Sally would tell me she had seen Matthew walking behind me, mimicking my footsteps and holding his head down with his hands behind him. Kids are imitators, and it's great when they imitate genuine faith!

4. *Take advantage of everyday opportunities to involve youngsters in discussions that help their faith in God to grow.* Sometimes we mistakenly believe that children are incapable of thinking about faith. Sometimes we restrict our conversations to childish matters and don't offer them a chance to learn or practice critical thinking. I heard recently of a young couple's three-year-old who was asked to tell in his own words what happened to Jonah when the prophet refused God's call to preach in Nineveh. The youngster was a strong-willed little guy who was sent to his room frequently because of his misbehavior. Without missing a beat, this three-year-old said of Jonah, "God had to give him a time-out." He was essentially correct! Kids often understand more than we realize.

It's important to discuss everyday matters at home with our children, especially those that come up in school. Often the way to disciple children and help them grow in their faith is to answer the questions that come up naturally in school. An alert dad can find ways to help his children explore their ideas about their faith and values at home, especially during mealtime.

One time we were visiting a farm and we saw a little dead animal. It was the first time my kids had seen anything dead. They were three and five years old. I used this as an opportunity to explain death and the afterlife to them; I wanted to pass on to them my faith in God for life eternal.

Take advantage of conflicts, disagreements, and stories about movie stars and sports heroes. Do we agree with the decisions they make? Do we think they are telling the truth? Why or why not? This is the time to inject biblical principles. This is how we model our faith for our children in a way that they can "catch it."

5. *Talk to your children about faith at a level they can comprehend.* Children up to the age of about eight are very concerned about justice, right and wrong, and following the rules even when they don't understand them. A young child's moral system is based on obedience. But from about 8-12 years old they begin to transition to more abstract, conceptual thinking. At that point we need to explain the reasons behind things. Why do the rules exist? We should encourage our children to ask questions even though we will continue to insist on obedience to family norms.

When a child is searching for meaning behind the rules and he asks, "Why should I do that?" he is not necessarily abandoning family values. Rather, he is challenging the rules in order to understand them. That's the natural process that God intends all of us to go through. We should not see this as a threat, but as an opportunity to teach our children and to help their faith grow and their minds become more discerning.

6. *Help your children gain a sense of faith from stories outside of their own experience.* These stories can be about contemporary people, biblical characters, or legendary heroes that help to inspire their faith.

Sally and I did this by telling stories about our missionary friends and their great exploits. We encouraged our children to read missionary biographies to help expose them to modern-day heroes of the faith.

7. *As children get older, encourage them to make their own decisions about their faith.* As your children make the transition from absolutes to concepts to questions, help them to think on their own. Don't just give information, but ask them to repeat it in their own words, analyze it, then finally synthesize it, apply it, and put it into their own value system.

8. *Get to know the values and the faith of your children's friends in order to better cope when they conflict with your own.* It's important to understand the faith of other people so we can help our kids anticipate the questions they will ask. If we don't take time to invite their friends over and become familiar with their beliefs or values (and thereby know how to respond to such), then our kids are going to think we are out of touch and that our faith is out of date.

We should never put our children in a position where they think that in order to believe one thing they must disrespect another. It's not a choice between our beliefs or disrespecting their friends. We want to encourage our kids to show respect and to realize there could be some good in what their friends believe, but that the whole truth is found in Christ alone.

9. *Spouses should try to agree on issues of faith so children aren't confused by conflicting views.* A dad should talk these issues over with his wife and they should strive to express the same faith and values. We shouldn't argue with one another or attack one another's ideas in front of the kids. Ideally we would work out our beliefs long before the kids arrive and be able to express those beliefs together in harmony.

10. *Tell your children you don't have all the answers, but you know where you can find them.* You can always go to God's Word and to other books and come back with an answer. Being honest is a very important part of helping your children grow in confidence in their faith. If we get nervous, insecure, and defensive when our kids ask questions, that's a sure sign that we haven't thought through our faith sufficiently to be able to pass it on to our children.

> *There is nothing like hands-on involvement to help children get excited. Involve your kids, and watch God use them!*

Our attitude is as important as the answers we give. It is important that we take the time to think through tough questions, perhaps do a little reading, and examine carefully the different viewpoints. Then in a rational, calm way, we can explain why we disagree with the beliefs of a Mormon or a Muslim or a Christian Scientist or an atheist. It's crucial for our children's sake that we frequently restate and reemphasize our values and views.

## VITAL FAITH IN GOD

Duffy Robbins suggests we can take one of three approaches to help our child develop faith in God: guilt, goad or guide.[3]

*Guilt* says, "There are a lot of starving children in the world, and you should be a lot more grateful."

*Goad* says, "C'mon! If you don't do something, we will never do it. Aren't you ever going to want to do something for God?"

*Guide* says, "Hey, I'm going to go downtown and maybe go to a coffee shop in a different part of town just so I can meet some people from different backgrounds and cultures. Would you like to go with me? I'm praying that God will help me meet some interesting people."

Obviously, guiding is the best option. Sally and I regularly got our kids involved in praying with us for people to accept Christ. I sometimes took my children with me when I ventured out on the streets to talk with some poor soul in a church-sponsored outreach. Knees knocking and butterflies fluttering in our stomachs, we ventured out in faith, together. I wanted to get my children involved in the actual ministry process. There is nothing like hands-on involvement to help kids get excited, especially when God uses them in a special way. Faith at a time like this doesn't mean all our fears are gone, but it does mean we get involved so God can use us. Any one of us can do this—man, woman, or child!

Matthew and Misha found this out many years ago in a King's Kids outreach. Sally and I wanted to teach them that God could use them simply by praying blessings for people. We thought that the kids could do what kids do best, and that is to be childlike, honest, and to love people.

At one of the outreaches in the middle of downtown Amsterdam, a big crowd gathered as the King's Kids sang and shared their testimonies. After the event was over, we encouraged the kids to mingle within the crowd and ask people if they could pray for them. When a person said yes, the kids prayed a blessing for him or her in simple, childlike terms.

After the crowd had dispersed, Misha and Matthew and one other King's Kid walked up to a man on the street who looked terribly lonely. They asked him if they could pray for him. When he didn't say no, they went ahead and prayed for him. After they were done, that man in his own stumbling words asked God to forgive him and come into his life and help him.

It turned out this man was a backslidden Baptist preacher whose wife had divorced him, and he was thinking about committing suicide. He had wandered aimlessly to the square, where many adults had tried and failed to talk to him. He told us later he was hardened against adults. But these children caught his attention, won his heart, and earned a hearing. When our kids approached him, he listened to them and gave them a chance. They broke his heart when they prayed for him; their prayer pierced the walls he had built up and demolished his fear, and he recommitted his life to the Lord. Today, that man is back in the ministry.

## THE KEY TO BECOMING GOD'S MAN IN THE FAMILY

God can do this *and so much more* in our lives as men if we will just give Him the chance. If God can use a child, He can use us. If we will become childlike—if we will trust the Lord in spite of our fears, failures, and weaknesses—God can and will redeem our mistakes. He can redeem our failures and give us a brand-new beginning, just as He did with the Baptist preacher.

> *You're just exactly the right man for the job!*

If we have failed and are desperately aware that we have not been God's man, let me say that God wants to give us a new beginning. God *specializes* in new beginnings. He draws a line behind us at our heels and casts all of our sins and failures into the sea of His forgetfulness. As Corrie ten Boom said, He then puts up a sign that says, "No fishing here!"

God can create a new beginning for us. He is the Creator, and He has the right and the authority to create us anew. All of this He has made possible through Jesus dying on the cross for us to redeem our past and give us a new beginning.

Do you want to be God's man in the family? You can be, if you really want to. It takes committing yourself to live without compromise by the nonnegotiables God impresses upon your heart. Your nonnegotiables may be slightly different from mine, but what's important is that you live out those convictions which issue from your relationship to the living God. Commit to them! Write them down! Live by them! That's how you become God's man in the family.

In fact, if you consider Jesus Christ to be your Savior and Lord, I can say without hesitation that *you're just exactly the right man for the job!*

## ═══ *ACTION STEPS* ═══

- One of the most important nonnegotiables of all is to impart to your children a faith in God. In what ways is your faith on display to your children? Do your children see you following rules, or loving the Lord? What are some ways you can make the difference clear to them?

- An excellent way to cultivate faith is to allow your children opportunities to serve God. Through your church or as a family, plan and carry out a community project you could do together . . . such as a food basket or yard work for a shut-in, serving in a kitchen at a rescue mission, rounding up nice clothes you have outgrown and giving them to another family in need, and so on. Agree on a project everyone would like to do this month, and make it happen.

• Inviting your children to join you in prayer is a great exercise for their faith, for it allows them to observe God in action. Give each child a short list—perhaps three or four items—of things they can pray for on your behalf. Keep the prayer requests appropriate to the child's age level. Then as prayers are answered, share the news with your children. This will make an incredible impression on their lives.

# GUIDELINES FOR SELECTING A COUNSELOR

Unfortunately, there are unqualified individuals who prey on sincere Christians by calling themselves counselors. When in search of a counselor, it is important to make sure whomever you go to is well-qualified and is supportive of the Christian faith. Following are three basic guidelines you will want to use when choosing a counselor:

1. Get a referral from a respected and trusted church leader, family doctor, or Christian friend who has had previous contact with the counselor and knows him or her personally.

2. Competent counselors are not threatened if a prospective patient calls and tactfully asks about their qualifications, theoretical and biblical orientation, experience, and type of license they hold.

3. Fees should be discussed in advance of any counseling commitments.

# NOTES

### Chapter 1—What's a Man to Do?

1. Andrew Greeley, *Faithful Attraction* (New York: Tor Books, 1991), 21.
2. Nancy Gibbs, "Father," *Time* (June 28,1993), 53.

### Chapter 4—A Warm Man in a Cold World

1. Maureen Rank, *Dealing with the Dad of Your Past* (Minneapolis: Bethany House Publishers, 1990), 37.

### Chapter 6—Seven Keys for Releasing Your Kids

1. C.S. Lewis, *The Great Divorce* (New York: The Macmillan Company, 1946), 95.
2. Ibid., 96-97.

### Chapter 8—The Fun Doesn't Start Till the Fat Lady Sings

1. Kathy Peel and Jay Mahaffey, "Mom, I'm Bored. What Can I Do?" *Focus on the Family* (June 1989), 2.

### Chapter 10—Believing God for the Impossible

1. Duffy Robbins, *The Ministry of Nurture* (Grand Rapids: Zondervan, 1990), 54.
2. This material is adapted from an article by Norman Lobsenz, "The Values You Cherish," *Woman's Day* (November 22, 1979), 48ff.
3. Robbins, *The Ministry of Nurture*, 50.
4. Ibid., 221.

*Floyd McClung* is the director of Mission Village in Colorado. Mission Village is a leadership-training center and community where dedicated Christians actively share their faith, wisdom, and experience with those who desire to make an impact on the world for God. Mission Village also serves as a retreat, recreational, and retirement community where interested Christians can have their primary residence, own a vacation getaway, or make a long-term investment in extending God's kingdom.

Anyone interested in more information about Mission Village can call or write:

Mission Village
P.O. Box 5
Trinidad, CO 81082

(800) 222-9343
(719) 846-4555
FAX (719) 846-4363